KNIVES, SWORDS, & DAGGERS

BARNES & NOBLE BOOKS

NEW YORK

This edition published by Barnes & Noble, Inc.,
by arrangement with Book Sales, Inc.

2004 Barnes & Noble Books

This edition produced for sales in the U.S.A., its
territories, and dependencies only.

M 10 9 8 7 6 5 4 3 2 1

ISBN 0-7607-6226-0

This book was designed and produced by
Quintet Publishing Limited
6 Blundell Street
London N7 9BH

Designed and Edited by Q2A Solutions

Publisher: Ian Castello-Cortés
Associate Publisher: Laura Price
Creative Director: Richard Dewing

Art Director: Roland Codd
Project Editors: Jenny Doubt, Catherine Osborne

Manufactured in Singapore by Provision Pte Ltd
Printed in Singapore by Star Standard Industries (Pte) Ltd.

The material used in this publication previously appeared in
A Collector's Guide to Swords, Daggers & Cutlasses by Gerald
Weland and *Identifying Pocket Knives: The New Compact Study
Guide and Identifier* by Bernard Levine.

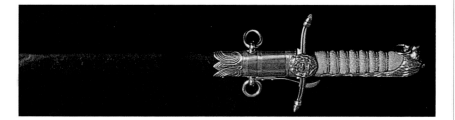

Contents

Introduction

An edged weapon may be defined as any implement designed for cutting, which possesses a blade more than twice as long as it is wide. Many weapons may be so defined because over the years the development and refinement of swords, daggers, and knives have led to a huge selection for collectors to choose from.

Modern warfare, when the opposing troops are rarely close enough to each other to make physical contact, has encouraged collectors of military memorabilia to recognize edged weapons as of a particular age and warfare style that makes them hugely collectible. A part of the reason for this growth in interest lies in the desire to invest in objects that will appreciate in value. In this respect, some collectors regard militaria as others might regard fine porcelain, paintings, or other works of art. Other collectors admire edged weapons for the skill and artistry with which they were made,

Right from top to bottom **A Royal Navy midshipman's dirk, dating from Victorian times; Prussian infantry officer's sword, c1900; Model 1889 Bavarian cavalry officer's sword; Third Reich Luftwaffe dagger, post-1937; British general officer's sword, dated 1831; Russian naval dirk from the era of Czar Nicholas II; and British armed forces World War I dirk.**

Left **A Viking sword hilt made of silver and gold. The handguard is reinforced and eloquently proves how seriously the Norsemen took their weaponry. This sword was most probably made in Finland.**

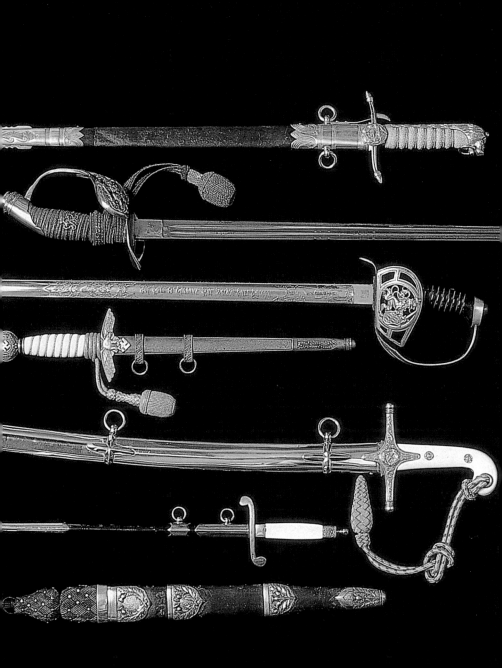

and acquire them merely for their visual appeal. The third type of collector appreciates the artistry of the knife or dagger as a tool.

However, few would dispute that the real attraction of edged weapons is that, unlike an Impressionist painting or a Royal Worcester teapot, a sword, dagger, or a knife allows the owner to "touch" history. Such weapons and tools represent the journey of mankind through the ages in a way that a stamp, a painting, or a piece of porcelain can never do.

Here, this journey is traced by examining the major types of edged weapons in terms of their historical position, their development through increased understanding of metallurgy, metal-working, military development, and fashion and style.

Right **German short sword with a broad curved blade, originally called a Dusagge; c1590-1610. An efficient weapon, this was used in naval combat as a cutlass.**

Left **A tenth century reconstruction of a Viking grave. Note that most of what the Viking took with him to Valhalla was weaponry. The hand would have been wrapped around the hilt of the sword when he was interred.**

Swords

The Parts of a Sword

The example below is specifically a naval cutlass, but the terms can be applied to any sword.

The Shoulder: Whether single-edged or double-edged, it was customary to leave up to six inches of the cutting edge unsharpened. This was advisable, just in case the user's hand slipped over the hand guard. On such weapons as rapiers or basket-hilted broadswords, the shoulder was frequently dispensed with.

The Edge: Also called the cutting edge, it was sharpened for use in battle. On most curved weapons, with the exception of some eighteenth century backswords, the edge is that which curves backward or upward.

The Tip

The Handle: The handle, or mount is, in this case, very plain. The knuckle guard and the hand guard are melded together to form one part. The tang button at the top of the hilt is negligible. There is but the slightest hint of a quillon.

The Blade

The Back Edge: It is the unsharpened edge on any single-edged weapon. Obviously, a double-edged weapon would not have a back edge.

The False Edge: It was almost never seen on a curved cutlass or saber. However, on some longer single-edged swords, it was customary to sharpen a few inches of the back edge as well in order to make the penetration and withdrawal easier while thrusting.

The Parts of a Handle

"Handle" is the correct generic term for this part of the sword, the example here being a British naval presentation sword. However, strictly speaking, it should be referred to as the "mount."

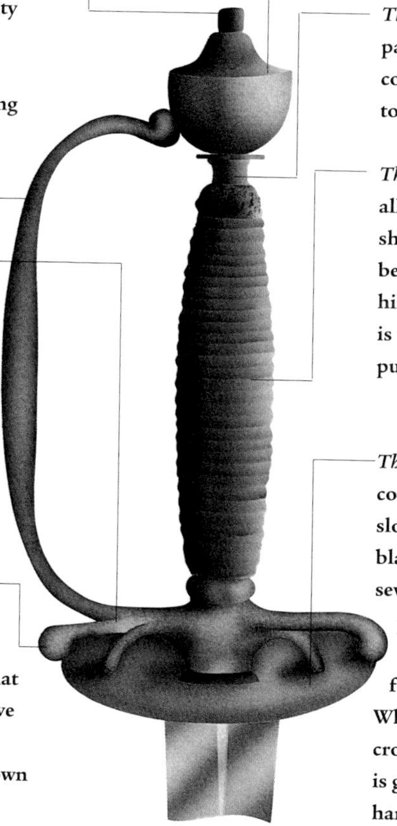

The Tang Button: **The tang button is found on some heavier or more elaborate swords, but rarely on knives. Adding stability and strength, it was inserted like a screw into the butt of the tang (inside the hilt).**

The Knuckle Guard

The Cross Guard: **The cross guard was designed to prevent slippage of the hand over the blade. This feature can be seen in the earliest of weapons.**

The Quillon: **In the case of rapiers, quillon frequently became so elaborate that they formed a protective basket hilt around the entire hand. Those shown here are very modest.**

The Pommel: **The pommel served to support the rear of the hand.**

The Hilt: **The hilt is that part of the weapon which covers the tang. It was used to hold the weapon.**

The Grip: **Though closely allied to the hilt, the grip should not be confused as being the same thing: some hilts had no grips. The grip is whatever covering was put on the hilt.**

The Ricasso: **A small, flat, or concave plate, containing a slot through which the blade is passed. It served several functions, primarily providing stability to the hilt and offering an area for ornamentation. When combined with the cross guard, it formed what is generally known as the hand guard.**

The Story of the Sword

The development of metal-working techniques is thought to have begun in Mesopotamia, sometime in 3500–3000 BCE. Copper was one of the earliest metals to be used by man. Today, its principal deposits are in the United States, Chile, Canada, Zambia, and Zaire, but in the early days, it was found in many parts of Europe and the Middle East.

The early Minoans (c 2900 BCE) are known to have fashioned implements from copper, gold, and silver. Archaeological excavations have also revealed that deposits of tin were used with copper to develop the earliest alloy known to man — bronze. While copper was used to make weapons, the discovery of bronze and its suitability for casting meant that, for the first time in history, strong blades of real length were able to be fashioned.

Below **A sword hilt of cast bronze with a green patina. The blade is missing, though the rivets for it remain. Danish, late Bronze Age (c 1200 BCE).**

Copper swords had once, in effect, been nothing more than long daggers. However, cast bronze blades, measuring 30–36in (75–90cm) in length, could be made from this fine-grained and malleable material. When prepared properly, bronze has a high tensile strength and offers considerable resistance to damage and corrosion. The shape of these early bronze swords also began to change, with a central rib being added to maintain maximum rigidity in thrusting.

During the third and second millennium BCE, migratory races, known today as People of the Sea, appeared in Europe. These people used metal, built impressive houses, traded with Crete and the islands of the Aegean, and settled in most of the Greek mainland. It is clear that these people were not Greek, and they may have actually come from southern Russia. These raiders made several innovations to the weaponry of the time. The type of warfare that they pursued made a sword as suitable for

cutting as it was for thrusting. They therefore developed a double-edged sword with a strong point, which could be used in either way.

Making weapons of this kind was difficult, however, because of the problems of attaching the tang to the hilt. When swords were nothing more than long knives, it was a simple matter to insert the rear of the blade into the handle and to hold it firm with a few small rivets. Forward and backward thrusting movements caused little structural strain, but swords that were intended for a broader range of strokes were more complicated to construct. This problem was solved by making a

Above **A stylized portrait of King Leonidas of Sparta. His 300 men held the Pass at Thermopylae against Persian invaders in 480 BCE.**

special groove in the tang, into which the shoulder, or rear, of the blade could fit snugly and tightly. Larger rivets held them together.

More efficient, of course, was to cast the blade and the tang as a single piece, but this practice does not appear to have been widely followed. This was partly because it would then be necessary to cover the handle with materials like wood or bone to provide a decent grip in battle. The

wood or bone would generally become dislodged, even after limited use, and could render the weapon useless — even in the hands of an expert swordsman. In addition, the primitive methods of construction made elaborate, one-piece weapons difficult to produce.

It would be wrong to believe that weaponry was standardized throughout Europe at this time, and that construction techniques were uniform. Long before the rise of the nation state, different groups of tribes struggled with each other for supremacy. It would appear that, even at this early stage, the techniques and designs of "military technology" were closely guarded secrets.

The introduction of iron brought further changes to sword construction,

Above The famous Bayeux Tapestry commemorating the Norman conquest of Britain. At the time, swords were used in a hacking technique.

for it was, of course, infinitely superior to bronze in many ways. Nevertheless, the two types of blade continued to coexist for several centuries. The Hittites, who had evolved in Asia Minor around 2000 BCE, had established a strong, centralized government by 1500 BCE. They appear to have been responsible for the great technological advances made in smelting iron. However, they do not seem to have benefited from this discovery in the making of weapons.

By 1200 BCE, the Hittite kingdom was gone, and was followed by the formation of empires that dominated

THE SWORD OF ROLAND

Feudal history springs to life in the long narrative poems known as *chansons de geste*, and one of the best known of these was the *Chanson de Roland*. Written in the eleventh century, this poem was devoted almost exclusively to describing fighting and feudal intrigue. It tells the story of Roland, a young French soldier who died in 778 at Roncesvalles during Charlemagne's invasion of Spain. Roland was actually killed by the Basques, but in the *Chanson de Roland*, the Saracens had become the enemy. The 4,000 lines of the *Chanson* state how Charlemagne sent Ganelon, Count of Mayence, and one of Charlemagne's Paladins, as an ambassador to Marsilius, the Pagan King of Saragossa. Inspired by jealousy, Ganelon betrayed to Marsilius the route that the Christian army planned to take on its return to France. Marsilius arrived at Roncesvalles just as Roland was conducting a rear-guard of 20,000 men. Roland fought until 100,000 Saracens were slain, and only 50 of his men survived. When another 50,000 from the enemy camp poured in, Roland blew his enchanted horn. Although Charlemagne heard him, Gamelon persuaded him that Roland was just hunting deer, thus leaving Roland to his fate.

Legend has it that Roland's sword, the Durandal (also Durindana or Duranda) had once belonged to Hector, but Roland had won it from a giant named Jutmundus. It had, in its hilt, a thread from the cloak of the Virgin Mary, a tooth of St Peter, one of St Denys's hairs, and a drop of St Basil's blood. According to the *Chanson de Roland*, after he was mortally wounded, Roland strove to break his sword on a rock, to keep it from falling into the hands of the Saracens. But because it was unbreakable, he hurled it into a poisoned stream, where it was destined to remain forever.

the Near East. The first of these was established by the Assyrians, who came from northern Mesopotamia to the east of the river Tigris. By 665 BCE, the Assyrians controlled the area from the southern frontier of Egypt, through Palestine, Syria, and much of Asia Minor, to the Persian Gulf in the southeast. The Assyrians are, in fact, often credited with having developed the sword as we know it today. In fact, their success in extending the frontiers of their empire was, in part, due to their use of iron weapons. Because iron is more common than copper or tin, it was possible for them to arm a greater number of men far more cheaply.

It was during the second millennium BCE that sheaths first appeared. When it was discovered that iron weapons could be sharpened to an edge previously unknown with bronze implements, it obviously became necessary to protect the blades — and the swordsmen — when the swords were not in use. Initially, the benefits that accrued from sheathing swords were marginal, for the early examples tended to be made of wood or even bronze. This meant that unsheathing and returning the blade to its resting place just a few times inflicted all kinds of damage to the edge. However, leather sheaths were developed and became

widespread by about 1000 BCE. These sheaths protected the blade, but left it undulled by sheathing.

Major developments in swordmaking took place over the next few centuries, between 900–500 BCE. Yet, even at this time, swords appear to have been regarded as much as art forms as they were weapons. Magnificent grips and intricate decoration seem to have been as important as effective blades.

Because iron increased tensile strength, blades were often more than 40in (1m) long, almost too long to be effectively wielded at a time when, according to archaeologists, a man standing 5ft 6in (1.7m) tall was considered to be robust! By the time Rome was founded in about 750 BCE, all the so-called barbarian tribes of Europe were using these long swords, although battle-axes and spears seem to have been the preferred weapons.

It was not until c500 BCE that these swords came to be regarded as weapons for combat. Most of the

Right **This excellent sixteenth century portrait shows Edward VI, son of Henry VIII, who died before reaching adulthood. Note the ear dagger, so popular with royalty at the time. Though the artist is unknown, the work is reminiscent of Hans Holbein, who painted much of English court life in that period.**

decoration vanished, and the emphasis shifted to the functional characteristics of the blade. Swords from this period are usually all described as "pre-Roman," although there were considerable regional differences in style.

One of our main sources of knowledge of weaponry, dating from around 500 BCE, is the La Tene site in France, where iron weapons have been found. It is clear that, by this time, the supremacy of iron over bronze for making weapons was widely recognized. Bronze was still used for gilt ornamentation, and sometimes for handles too, but it had otherwise completely fallen from use. Swords had started to decrease in length, and measures between 30-36in (75-90 cm). At this stage the first trademarks also seem to have been used, not only to identify which tribe a sword belonged to, but also where it was made.

Left **This portrait of Gautier de Chatillon depicts the invasion of Egypt in 1249, during the Crusades. During this campaign, King Louis IX was captured, and reached the Holy Land only after paying the proverbial king's ransom.**

Right **This extremely rare Italian medieval sword, with gilt pommel and cross guard, dates from c1400.**

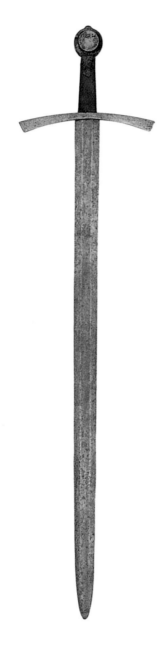

There were still major problems, however, even with iron swords. Repeated impact during battle frequently caused the handle to twist around the tang if improperly riveted. This proved to be a severe setback, especially when the foe comprised the extremely well-organized Roman legions, with their powerful Gladius swords! Eventually, of course, the Romans were defeated, and the long sword proved to be more effective, especially when it was used on horseback to cut rather than thrust. As the Roman Empire began to give way in the third century BCE, the long sword gained supremacy, and it remained essentially unchanged until the period of Charlemagne.

By the early Middle Ages, swords became, if not longer, at least bulkier. By this time, grips were adorned with ornamentation, often being inlaid with precious metals, or with pearls or other expensive materials. Yet, because the sword was so large, if a blow was forcefully delivered, the sword was difficult to hold, and the combatant either dropped his weapon or, worse, his hand slipped down the unsharpened shoulder, on to the blade itself. It was here that the quillon made its appearance. This was, in essence, a hand guard between the grip and the shoulder of the blade. Originally, the quillon was a

Far Left Dating from 1360, this rare medieval sword (of unknown origins) has a long blade measuring 33in (84cm).

Right A number of interesting features adorn this Scottish military presentation sword, which dated from 1807. Note the finely etched trophies, lion's head crest, the motto "*Semper Fidelis*," and the personal inscription.

Bellum ihi Gwidi de Tu

single, straight bar, and was often called the cross guard; later, it became more elaborate, curving back toward the pommel on the rear of the grip, and forming what was known as the counterguard. The quillon, thus, not only made it almost impossible to lose the grip on a weapon, but also protected the hand from injury.

Throughout the early Middle Ages, advances continued to be made in the design of swords, most improvements being made in the area now known as France. Grips became more defined and elaborate, and the pommel at the rear began to show curves and gilded decoration. The blades, however, continued to be used only for cutting or, more accurately, hacking. In folklore, literature, art, and practice, the preferred technique was to strike the opponent with an overpowering stroke. Contemporary references almost always allude to "hewing" the foe with one masterful stroke.

In the days of chivalry and romance, a knight's sword and his

Left **German and Italian knights fighting in the fourteenth century. The exact campaign is vague, but it undoubtedly concerned one of the interminable series of struggles between the German Hohenstaufen dynasty and the Papacy, which wracked Europe for several centuries.**

horse were his two most highly prized possessions, and it was customary to give each a name. Among the most famous such swords are Balmung, one of the swords made by Wieland for Siegfried; Courtain, the short sword of Cigier the Dane; Tizona, the sword of El Cid; and, perhaps the most famous of all, Excalibur, the sword of King Arthur. In particular, the preoccupation with swords and swordsmanship revealed in the *chansons de geste* tells us much about

Top A scene from the Battle of Aljubarrota, Iberia, in 1385, showing men at arms dueling with two-handed swords. In this battle, Portuguese ruler John I triumphed with English help, thereby repulsing a Spanish invasion. This led to the signing of the Treaty of Windsor between England and Portugal, in May 1386. The treaty is still enforced today.

Below Left Late sixteenth century sword (probably German) with a hilt richly chiseled, silvered, and gilt. The Renaissance influence on this sword is evident in its great weight, its length of 35in (89cm), and its ornamentation.

Below An Italian knight's sword, c1460, with a hilt of gilt bronze. Similar weapons, though iron-mounted, have been excavated near the site of the battle of Castillon (1453), in France.

Right *Fight for the Standard* a scene from the American Civil War by an unknown artist. Early in this conflict, Confederate cavalry consisted of vastly superior horsemen, though by the time of Gettysburg in 1863, matters had blanced out considerably.

Below A Model 1889 Bavarian cavalry officer's sword. These were in service right through the early days of World War I, though the Germans were among the first to realize the deadly nature of the machinegun, and abandon cavalry warfare. The hinged guard allows it to lie flat. The lion emblem, whether facing, recumbent, or rampant, was historically a popular motif for most European countries.

Above Early seventeenth century sword for cavalry use, bearing on its blade the marks of Wolfgang Stantler, a Munich bladesmith. The wide, double-edged blade is unusual for a cavalry weapon.

the attitudes to chivalry and the knightly life prevailing in eleventh and twelfth century France.

The period between the thirteenth and early fourteenth centuries is generally regarded as the zenith of sword craftsmanship, both in terms of function and beauty. Grips were engraved and inlaid, and pommels were large and highly decorated. Moreover, the cross guards above the shoulder of the blade were often so large and sturdy that they made the sword look more like a cross than a weapon. Throughout southern and western Europe there was a preference for blades that were efficient thrusting weapons, although elsewhere cutting blades remained dominant. All this changed in the mid-fourteenth century, however, after the Battle of Crécy (1346).

This early battle of the Hundred Years' War (1337–1453), in which Edward III of England defeated the forces of Philip VI of France, was a watershed in military history. The English longbowmen overcame the massed cavalry ranks of the French, and though medieval chroniclers are notoriously unreliable, it is reported that no fewer than 1,542 French noblemen and knights perished together with some 20,000 others.

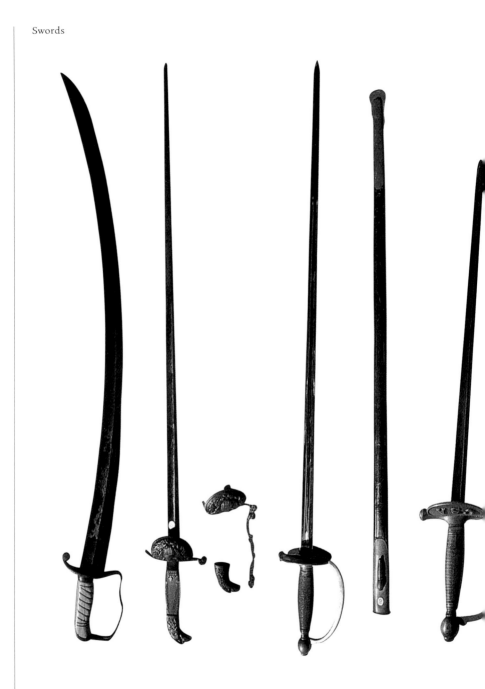

Armies suddenly became larger and more mobile, and, while it was difficult to find quantities of good longbowmen, contingents of able-bodied men who could wield a sword could be found easily. Soon, the use of swords had proliferated such that they were being issued *en masse* to infantry throughout the fifteenth and sixteenth centuries. These swords were invariably double-edged, sturdy, and sharply pointed, to make them effective jabbing instruments.

Only after the sword-bearing infantry was sent to attack the enemy, was the cavalry deployed to exploit the breaches in the line and, in theory, to rout the foe. As a consequence, the sword that had been familiar to the knightly class for

Left A selection of nineteenth and early twentieth century American swords.

Left to Right A sturdy weapon made by the Ward and Bartholomew Company of Connecticut, which died out in the early 1800s; an artillery officer's sword, dating from 1821, with rococo knuckle guard, and regular eagle-carved pommel; a sword phased out in 1835, issued to artillery officers of state militia; based on a French type, an American NCO sword specified by the War Department in 1840; Confederate NCO sword, probably belonging to an infantryman from the Civil War era.

several years, became outmoded and useless. It was then that the cavalry sword began to evolve. The blade was either long and slender, or short and broad, depending on the type of armaments expected to be used by the enemy. Soon, a distinctive type of weapon appeared, the specialized sword known today as the saber. Although firearms were increasingly used by the mid-eighteenth century, the saber survived and remained in use until World War I.

Right **More swords dating from after the War of Independence.**

Left to Right **A standard weapon manufactured between 1790 and 1810; based on the 1822-pattern British cavalry saber, this weapon was made for a special force of dragoons, formed in March 1833; the Musician Sword, adopted by the United States in 1840 to fulfill a support function in battle; standard French-style weapon, carried by United States artillery from 1833 until c1870; authorized for use in 1860, this variant on the standard officer's sword was useless for real battle, being too short and frail; sword issued to medical officers during the Civil War; this foot officer's sword was based on a French design.**

The American Civil War

One myth that has evolved suggests that there was something special about the armaments used during the American Civil War. It is true that advances in firepower and signaling were made, but there was, in fact, little that qualified as new, which is also the case for the edged weapons that were used.

The cavalry saber used by the American dragoons to snatch the western United States from Mexico in the 1840s was essentially the same weapon used during the Civil War and later against the Native American tribes. In 1840, the War Department adopted a non-commissioned officer's sword based on an 1822 French model. Although this was handsome and graceful to look at, it was actually a cumbersome and poorly balanced weapon. Even so, it not only saw service in every war from the 1840s, but was also in use in the United States as late as the 1930s.

Confederate weapons were made in so many places that it is impossible to catalog all the manufacturers. Many were made by village blacksmiths, and

Left **During the American Revolution, it was rarer for infantry to fight with swords than for cavalry — but it did occur. This protarait by John S. Copley shows the death of a British officer, Major Pierson.**

35

the Confederate forces were faced with the joint problems of few and poor-quality weapons. Many were imported, especially from the United Kingdom, where one of the major suppliers was the Mole Company of Birmingham.

Federal swords were designed for appearance as well as effectiveness. They were used to designate rank and, often, the branch of service. The sword and the sword belts were expected to be worn at all times when on duty, and suspended from a special hook attached to the belt when the soldier was on foot.

General officers were issued with a straight sword with a gilt hilt, silver grip, and brass or steel scabbard. Almost all other officers were to own a simpler sword, based on the War Department's 1850 pattern. The General Order 21 of August 1860 extended the wearing of swords to other personnel. Medical and pay departments were to wear a small sword and scabbard, based on the pattern designated by the Surgeon-General's Office. Meanwhile, the officers of volunteer cavalry regiments were to adopt the cavalry saber and scabbard then in use.

A sword based on the 1850 pattern was also ordered for all men of all ranks in the artillery and infantry, although few riflemen ever

actually saw one. Other branches, such as the engineers, also had prescribed swords, as did the army musicians, who acted as stretcher-bearers on the battlefield.

According to the Ordnance Manual of 1861, 10 types of sword were officially in use, nine of which were approximately 40in (1m) long, including the handle when scabbarded. In reality, though, Federal officers wore swords of almost unlimited variety, and no great effort was ever made to enforce the regulations. Field officers of all services who wanted a real weapon continued to use a version of the 1850 pattern sword, while a light saber based on a French pattern was adopted for use by artillerymen in 1840. However, despite being an attractive and useful weapon, this light saber was not widely worn, and remained in service for 50 years. Artillery officers wore swords like those of the enlisted men, but were distinguished because their weapons generally displayed modest decoration on the hilt, or even on the shoulder of the blade.

Right **The surrender of General Lee in New Jersey during the American Revolution, after Washington abandoned New York in 1776. The man accepting the sword is reputedly Colonel Banastre Tarleton.**

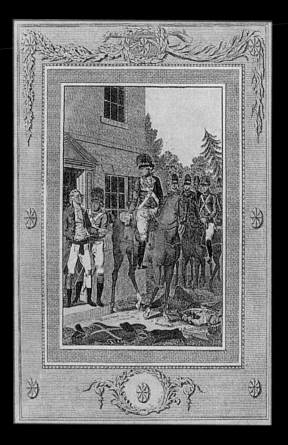

The most famous sword from this period is the cavalry saber. This was, essentially, the Federal weapon first issued in 1840, and one that was based on a version of a French pattern first adopted in 1822. The American version was nicknamed the "old wristbreaker," which suggests its main shortcoming. In 1860, a lighter saber with a more narrow blade was introduced, although the two versions are difficult to distinguish at first glance. Many of the swords were purchased during the Civil War, with at least 11 firms contracted to supply the Federal cavalry. Most often seen these days are those made by the J.T. Ames Co. of Chicopee, Massachusetts, known as the Ames pattern.

As far as the collection of Confederate swords is concerned, the weapons most often seen are the infantry officers' sword, the non-commissioned officers' sword, and the cavalry saber. Most of the

Left **General Philip Sheridan leading the successful charge of his cavalry at Cedar Creek, during his Valley Campaign of 1864. Though "Little Phil" barely got through West Point because of an assault on a senior cadet, he proved to be one of the most dashing, if cold-blooded, of American cavalrymen.**

1760

infantry officers' swords would be the 1850 pattern (if its owner was a defector from the Federal Army), or a variant on it made by a southern blacksmith. Some would be imports from the Mole Company, or other United Kingdom-based suppliers. The non-commissioned officers' swords and cavalry sabers are less common, although they occasionally appear at auctions. It is sometimes difficult to identify them precisely, because the decoration on many of them is misleading or meaningless. In general, the number of Confederate weapons available to collectors is less than that of Union weapons, partly because fewer were made and partly because they were less well made, and have therefore not survived.

A collector is more likely to build up a good collection of Union weapons. Staff and field officers' swords are not that difficult to find, provided that one is persistent. Most would bear the date 1860, because of General Order 21, and were probably worn by officers of the United States Volunteers. The 1850 pattern is more difficult to find.

Left **During the American Revolution, the British cavalry were regarded as elite units. This man is carrying the standard short musket and a routine version of the cavalry broadsword.**

Almost all the officers' swords from the Union seem to be available in present times. It is even possible to find medical staff swords as well as some of its more interesting versions, such as the pre-1850 light artillery sword, which was based on the French pattern.

Many versions of the saber are also available, including the old Horseman's saber, which dates back to the beginning of the nineteenth century. Other contractors who supplied weapons are the so-called Rose Contract of 1811 and the Starr Contract of 1812–18, who supplied weapons that may have been used against Native Americans and the British. A few may even have been carried by members of the United States Volunteers. Versions of the "old wristbreaker" can also be found, as can the lighter, 1860 version, and some of the variants on it that were produced up to 1913.

Swords at Sea

Naval history began in the Middle East, around 3000 BCE, when crude river-going crafts were first constructed. By about 1200 BCE, the first battle fleets were assembled. However, the first-known naval actions, though sporadic and barely meriting the description of "battles," took place during the Greco-Trojan

War, sometime around 1180 BCE. The first naval battle that can be positively identified as such occurred in 571 BCE, and was fought between Carthage and Phoenicia.

During these early maritime battles, naval warfare was largely conducted by emulating land tactics as closely as possible. The Romans depended largely on an implement known as the *corvus* (grapnel). This was a long ramp with a spike on the underside, which could be dropped onto the deck of an enemy warship, effectively skewering it and therefore allowing a charge of Roman marines to capture the vessel. Roman soldiers went into battle aboard ships just as if they were serving with legions on land. Their equipment, too, varied little, although their cloaks were green, while their land-based equivalents wore red.

For centuries, naval weapons were similar to those in service on land, and it was not until the middle of the seventeenth century that

Left **The victorious charge of the American 2nd Dragoons at the Battle of Resaca de la Palma, in May, 1846. This defeat repelled Mexican invaders from Texas soil; never again would they occupy any part of American terrain. The victory was the climax of the campaign that brought Zachary Taylor to the White House.**

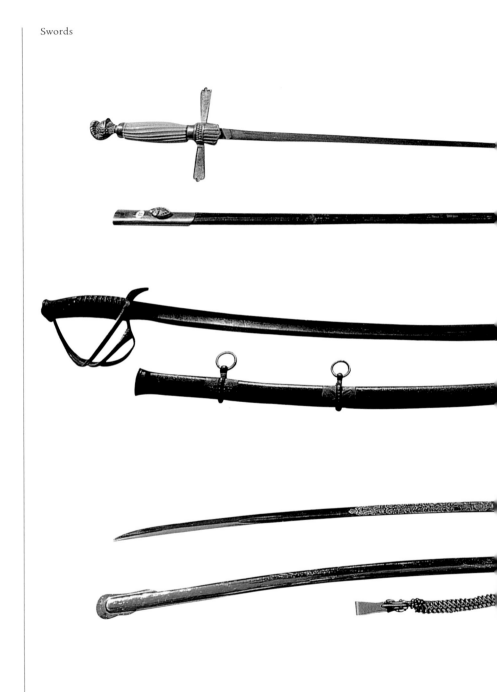

distinctive differences in armament appeared, and a tradition of naval weaponry began to emerge. The rise of distinctive naval weaponry appears to be in conjunction with, and perhaps a manifestation of, the rise of professionalism in national navies during the mid-seventeenth century. There is, of course, a well-established brotherhood of the sea, which does not seem to have had its equivalent among land-based forces. Advances and improvements in weaponry were adopted and copied almost as soon as they had occurred. Naval traditions, therefore, tended to overlap and advance simultaneously, and at first, there was little to differentiate between the weaponry used by

Left Top **This NCO sword was made during 1850 — 1870, and was the standard weapon for the American state militia at the outbreak of the Civil War.**

Middle **A standard Confederate infantry officer sword. It may well be the easiest Confederate Civil War weapon to collect, as it was made in substantial numbers.**

Bottom **In 1902, the United States Army ordered a new officer sword based on the cavalry saber. The blade was single-edged and slightly curved, usually not longer than 30in (76cm), and less than 1in (2.5cm) wide at the hilt.**

different countries. This was especially true of the edged weapons employed by Britain and the United States, although after the War of Independence, American swords tended to follow French styles more closely. Nevertheless, distinguishing the country of origin of early naval weapons is far from straightforward.

Most national armies achieved uniformity of clothing and armaments before their naval counterparts, but navies soon followed suit. Naval uniforms were adopted in France, and later in Spain, about 50 years before they were introduced into the Royal Navy, although a considerable degree of uniformity in dress and equipment had already occurred. The beginning of the reorganization of the Royal Navy is often credited to Charles II, and many reforms were introduced by his successor and brother, James II. This reorganization was completed by William Pitt the

Left **Perhaps the most famous of Elizabeth I's "sea dogs" was Sir Francis Drake, pictured here by an anonymous artist, a few years before the Spanish Armada. Note the incredibly long rapier with the onion-shaped knob and wire-plaited hilt. It is easy to see why the smaller and more manageable smallsword soon superseded it.**

Younger, in time for the French Revolutionary Wars.

The eighteenth century dawned with the War of the Spanish Succession (1701–1713), Louis XIV's final attempt to unite the throne of France with that of Spain. This war, which ranged Britain, Austria, the Netherlands, Portugal, and Denmark against France, Spain, and Bavaria, gave a tremendous impetus to the development of all kinds of weaponry. In the early part of the eighteenth century, boarding and capturing enemy vessels were also major naval objectives. This was partly because cannons were still of dubious value, and could not be guaranteed to inflict sufficient damage on an enemy warship to disable it. Another reason was that seizing a prize came to be considered an admirable accomplishment in its own right. Even if the captured ship could not be incorporated into the national fleet, which was often the case, the vessel could be dismantled and sold off to pay for some of the expenses of the successful navy.

In addition, many European countries adopted the view that the officers' role was to attain a foothold on an enemy vessel. In English-speaking countries, the prevailing view seemed to be that officers should lead their men into the thick of a fray

Left Issued in the 1890s to officers of the
Revenue Service, this is commonly known
as the cutter sword.

Far Left The standard American Navy
cutlass of the Civil War, first adopted in
1860 and modeled after a French style.
These weapons were found stored on older
American warships, as late as the 1930s.

and triumph by example. A naval
officer, compelled to lead an
onslaught across an enemy deck, thus
needed a weapon that was both
prestigious and functional.

Despite what is often portrayed in
films, individual swordfights at the
time were virtually unknown. As the
century progressed, however, hand-
to-hand fighting at sea became more
common, and naval officers began to
look for serviceable edged weapons.
Blades had to be of steel or iron, and,
as steel was more expensive, iron was
more widely used, especially as
increasing numbers of edged
weapons had to be supplied during
the wars of the late eighteenth and
early nineteenth centuries. The
handle, known at sea as the mount,
was generally made of brass, although
in the interests of economy, was
sometimes made of iron.

The first weapon widely adopted
by naval officers was a version of the
smallsword. It soon proved
inadequate, being chiefly effective

TYPES OF NAVAL UNIFORMS.

only for thrusting. The blade was too short, and fighting on a pitching, yawing deck required a much longer and more efficient weapon. Smallswords remained regulatory in the Spanish Navy for several generations, but elsewhere, a weapon known as the hanger quickly came to be almost universally adopted, especially among naval officers.

At first, hangers had comparatively short blades, but they steadily became longer. At the same time, there was a vogue for decorating blades with devices appropriate to the naval service, and it is from the longer and well-engraved hangers that the standardization of naval blades, or fighting swords, can be traced.

Hangers were initially more for adornment than anything else. They were frequently called hunting swords, because they were often decorated with scenes of fox hunting. The hunting sword seems to have moved from sea to land during the seventeenth century. The French developed the sword, turning it into a slightly curved, single-edged blade with a tapering grip. It achieved its greatest popularity in America, and

Left **Various dress uniforms of officers in the Royal Navy, c1890. By this time, of course, the sword was strictly a ceremonial object.**

one such weapon that belonged to George Washington may be seen at the Smithsonian Institution, in Washington DC.

This version of the hanger remained popular at sea throughout the era of the French Revolution, although the style of decoration changed with the adoption of national and naval motifs. First the mounts and then the blades began to be ornamented with a range of devices symbolizing the maritime profession.

In countries with a greater land mass, such as France, Russia, and Spain, army weapons had more influence over naval armaments than in island or coastal countries. Even so, the British Board of Ordnance, which was controlled by the army, held sway over the supply of almost all combat weapons to both services. Thus, it was not until the French Revolutionary Wars that the blade, which today is identified most closely with naval forces, came into existence.

On both sides of the Atlantic, a lightweight sword with a slightly curved blade and large hand guard resembling a seashell was soon widely

Right **The capture of the USS *Chesapeake* by a British vessel off Boston, on 1 June 1813. The officer is shown using a full-length sword, though the fallen man beneath him has a cutlass to hand.**

Right A French sailor of the Napoleonic era, carrying an ornate cutlass. Such weapons were generally only issued as needed for battle, and never for dress purposes, as portrayed here.

Left Marine Corps swords are much more scarce than other types, though they never existed in large quantities. Portrayed here is of the 1875 pattern. The blade length was usually 27–28in (68.5–71cm), with "USMC" etched on the blade.

used. The British Army ordered a new type of lightweight saber for the cavalry in 1796, and by 1805 it was copied by British seamen. As early as 1799, American sailors insisted that this weapon be made available to them and within a few years, this weapon — the cutlass — was accepted as standard in almost every major naval establishment.

Ironically, although the cutlass is undisputedly the best known naval edged weapon of all time, it enjoyed a comparatively brief period in favor. Battles by boarding parties were becoming a thing of the past. A few did occur during naval conflicts in the early 1800s, but by the mid-nineteenth century sword fighting was no longer a realistic part of naval warfare. The main reasons for this included the development of exploding shells, iron hulls, and

THE SWORD KNOT

By the end of the seventeenth century, fitting a length of cord to the mount of a sword had become popular at sea. One end of the cord was usually looped over the pommel, while the other end was wound around the wrist, so that if the sword was dropped in the midst of battle, it could quickly be retrieved.

By about 1750, sword knots used in the Royal Navy were blue and gold. Other nations gradually adapted them, selecting colors that were appropriate to the individual service. Eventually, the cord was replaced by gilded wire, which was not only more esthetically appealing, but also stronger.

Although sword knots had been worn by both military personnel and civilians in Britain for years, there were no regulations pertaining to their style in the Royal Navy, as they were considered to be nothing more than ornaments. However, they steadily became more decorative, and by the Napoleonic wars, even included tassels. By 1820, the sword knot was an established part of the Royal Navy uniform and, by 1827, was enforced by regulation.

The same general trend was followed in America. The blue and gold motif that is still used was quickly adopted, although the use of sword knots was never as widespread as in Britain. In some other European countries, especially Germany, however, they came to be regarded as marks of distinction, and were used to indicate both military achievement, and social status.

steam propulsion, all of which helped to make the need for naval swordfights obsolete.

However, the short, curved blade of the cutlass remained a common weapon, for example, for assassins in the Far East and South America.

Right **Press gangs recruited personnel for both the British Army and Navy. The soldier at right is identified as a regimental sergeant, but he seems to be carrying an officer's sword with pronounced pommel, stirrup knuckle guard, and gilt-wire wrapping on the grip.**

Types of Swords

From the rapier to the spadroon there is a huge variety of sword styles, most of which are of interest to collectors. Some types of sword are almost certainly beyond the reach of the average collector because of their rarity, but nonetheless are included here.

Bearing Sword

Bearing swords were never actually worn. Rather, they were made for ritual use at official ceremonies. This tradition is believed to have originated during the Byzantine Empire in the early seventh century. An arms bearer would carry an unsheathed sword, and point it upward in testimony to the power and prestige of the ruler behind whom he walked.

Bearing swords generally had wide blades, and were shaped like an isosceles triangle. They were covered in inscriptions that indicated the purity and nobility of the ruler. Their hilts were normally bronze, while the scabbards were traditionally covered in red velvet. Little wonder, then, that bearing swords could hardly have been of much value as weapons!

Long after two-handed swords were deemed worthless in battle, they were still manufactured by specialist craftsmen for ceremonial purposes. The assortment of bearing swords on display at festivals, tournaments of arms, royal weddings, funerals, and

Left A sword of Justice or "heading sword," used for executions; German, c1540. Anne Boleyn was executed by such a weapon in 1536.

Above The notorious Ku Klux Klan rose in the American South to frustrate the Union conquerors and the assimilation of freed slaves into society. They were a militant organization, and many leaders carried such weapons as a badge of fraternalism and rank.

so forth must have been dazzling. Bearing swords were especially popular in southern Europe, although their popularity began to spread throughout the continent from the eleventh century.

The largest bearing sword in existence is in the Armoury of the Tower of London. It belonged to Edward, Prince of Wales (later King Edward V, one of the Princes in the Tower). The German-bladed sword was made in 1475, when Edward was created the Duke of Chester.

Coronation Sword

The most elaborate of all swords is undoubtedly the coronation sword. Such a weapon symbolized the authority of a monarch and it therefore was impressive by necessity.

The most magnificent example is reputed to have been one that was worn by Charlemagne, when he was crowned the Holy Roman Emperor by Pope Leo III on Christmas Day in 800 CE. It was probably Charlemagne who also initiated the tradition of having the coronation sword blessed by the reigning pontiff.

Coronation swords were functional only in that they were modeled on the weapons in use at the time. Their primary role was to represent the grandeur of the monarchy. The goldsmiths, craftsmen, and armorers who worked on them turned them into works of art, rather than weapons.

Few coronation swords exist today. The most valuable and famous example is the sword used in the

coronations of French monarchs since the twelfth century. This rare archetype can be seen on display at the Louvre Museum in Paris, France.

Papal

Papal sword – this was the name given to the long-bladed weapons used by pontiffs as a sign of respect for military leaders whom they judged to be worthy. The custom began in the early eleventh century and was followed assiduously for many centuries.

The last such weapon was presented in 1823 by Pope Leo XII to the French Duke of Angoulême, for capturing the Trocadero forts guarding Cadiz, and so terminating a revolt against the Spanish king, Ferdinand VI.

Although Papal swords were usually presented to individuals, in 1511, Pope Julius II awarded one to Switzerland in recognition of the loyalty and valor of the Swiss Guards, the elite military group who still protect the pontiffs to this day.

Like bearing swords, papal swords had broad, double-edged blades, which were suitably impressive, but otherwise useless. They were often heavily inscribed with religious exhortations. Such swords were accompanied by a dome-shaped cap, on which was embroidered the

figure of a dove, symbolizing the Holy Ghost.

Because of their enormous intrinsic value, papal swords were often stolen, dismantled, or melted down. Only a handful of papal swords are still extant, most of which are in collections in Italy.

Presentation Sword

Presentation swords are closely related to bearing swords, but differ in that recipients of presentation swords would have generally earned them, rather than simply inherited

Above **An example of a presentation weapon — the Masonic Sword.**

Left **The Union army presented a variety of swords to men who performed heroic deeds during the Civil War. These were not intended for combat, of course, and are called GAR (Grand Army of the Republic) swords.**

them because of rank through birth or marriage. Presentation swords were symbols of honor, bestowed upon ranking members of the aristocracy and other like subjects, who had earned recognition by way of military prowess or political service.

The tradition is believed to have begun in Italy in the tenth century, when the sword presented was usually heavy. By the eighteenth century, a lighter version was more common. These swords were not, of course, intended to be used. Instead, they merely symbolized the appreciation of a monarch or a nation for services rendered; they were gaudy rather than useful, with the finest swordmakers, jewelers, and engravers employed to produce these works of art.

Several examples may be seen in museums around the world. Russia once had the largest collection of presentation swords in the world.

It was a long-established tradition for tsars to award such swords to Cossacks as rewards for bravery. Eventually, almost every officer in the Russian army had received a similar sword, often with gold inlaid inscriptions.

Presentation swords are frequently offered for sale at auctions. Among the most prized are Lloyd's swords, dating from the early nineteenth century, and American weapons of the same period that were presented to men for outstanding service in the Union army during the Civil War (these are known as Grand Army of the Republic, or GAR, swords).

While presentation, papal, coronation, and bearing swords represent the ultimate in swords as works of art, they are not weapons in the true sense.

Backsword

Similar to the modern saber, the backsword had a straight or slightly curved blade with a single edge. The blade was kept as short as possible, which allowed the sword to be wielded with one hand without impeding its effectiveness. Moreover, the sword could be rolled, so that blows could be efficiently delivered from either the forehand or the backhand stroke.

Today, the backsword is rarely identified as such. Examples are more likely to be known by the pattern year, style, function, and nationality of its group. However, the backsword remains among the most common of all swords.

Near Left This infantry officer sword, adopted under 1821 regulations, was a return to a straight-bladed backsword, though the length remained at something over 30in (76cm). It can be spotted easily because of the beads on the knuckle guard and the carved eagle on the pommel.

Far Left The United States Army infantry officer sword, which saw service in the War of 1812. This backsword had a broad, curved blade with a single edge, and is around 30in (76cm) long.

Diagonal An American artillery officer backsword dating from the early nineteenth century. The blade was usually single-edged, curved, and around 32in (80cm) in length. The pommel was generally hollow and carved with the image of an eagle.

Bastard Sword

The bastard sword is one weapon that has been misunderstood for centuries, merely on the basis of its name. The sobriquet originated from the fact that the sword could be used in a variety of ways. It is generally better known amongst collectors as the "hand-and-a-half" sword.

Not especially exotic, the bastard sword had a long, straight blade and a rounded pommel. The grip was sufficiently long, so that it could be wielded by both hands, in an overlapping grasp not dissimilar to that adopted when gripping a golf club. This allowed the combatant to increase the impact of any blow. Many people believe that the sword was one of the most effective and, without doubt, the most versatile, long-bladed weapon ever developed.

Bastard swords show up frequently at auctions and other sales. They are often sold for their historic interest rather than any inherent generic value. Because of this, auction catalog descriptions tend to be rather vague.

Right This "hand-and-a-half" sword is probably from Schloss Ambras in the Tyrol. The blade bears the mark of the late-sixteenth century swordsmith, Melchior Diefstetter of Munich.

Broadsword

The name broadsword is another name that causes confusion. Many broadswords are mistaken for the two-handed swords used in the Middle Ages, but true broadswords bear no relationship to the ones that most imagine Macbeth to have wielded. The broadsword had a straight, wide, and single-edged blade, and by the seventeenth century, it was widely accepted as the standard military sword, replacing the rapier as the common soldier's weapon. The broadsword usually featured a basket-type hilt and, when owned by the wealthy or powerful, it was often intricately decorated.

Broadswords from all countries and periods can be found: if a sword is from the English Civil War, the American War of Independence, or a host of other conflicts, it is almost certainly either a backsword or a broadsword. Broadswords are generally sturdier with larger hand guards. However, only experts would be able to distinguish the two.

Right A standard broadsword carried by most American officers during the American Revolution. However, it was also popular with British officers, and this one bears British regimental markings. The blade was generally around 25–27in (63–69cm) long and the swords were customarily decorated with pommels shaped as various animal heads.

Far Right A basket-hilted broadsword that dates from before the American Revolution (1775).

Claymore

The claymore was the two-handed sword of ancient Scotland whose name derives from the Gaelic term, *claidheamh mór*, meaning "great sword." The claymore became widespread only in the fifteenth and sixteenth centuries, but its forerunner existed for several centuries before then. At the time, the sword had a long, heavy blade, a straight grip, and a relatively small pommel. Several large quillons were also present in order to prevent the user's hands from slipping down beyond the shoulder. These quillions were essential, as claymores were usually employed with tremendous force. Only rarely were claymores ornamented, as they were primarily designed to be battle weapons.

Claymores are frequently confused with a Venetian weapon known as the schiavona, a name originating from the word *schiavoni*, which means "hired soldier". Since the seventeenth century, Scottish weapons tended to be based on the Italian sword, although there is, in reality, little resemblance between the two. Today, claymores are extremely rare and are only likely to be found in a sale of an aristocratic collection by one of the major auction houses.

Épée

Épées are probably best known as one of the blades used in the sport of fencing. However, this incarnation is a comparatively recent one. Originally, the épée was a stiff, heavy weapon with a blade that weighed 30oz (750g) or more. This may sound negligible, but in combination with the shape of the blade, which, in cross-section, was triangular, the épée was an impressive-looking weapon. The sword was used to establish the modern sport of fencing, and the movements for its proper employment were first described by the Italian swordmaster Achille Marozzo in his book, *Il Duello*.

Épées are excellent for parrying and thrusting, and are generally the kind of swords that one sees in adventure movies. In fact, épées were not useful in battle, as it was almost impossible to use them to inflict a serious wound. Like the rapier, the épée eventually became nothing more than an ornamental blade.

Right **A Highlander in action. Judging by the uniform of the dismounted cavalryman with whom he is dueling, this painting probably represents an event during the Cromwellian period of the seventeenth century.**

Gladius

Throughout the expansion of the grand Roman Empire, the gladius was the standard infantry weapon of the Roman legions. In fact, the word "gladiator" derives from the gladius, although only a few in the gladiator arena perished by it.

The gladius was a short, double-edged stabbing sword with a sharp point. The blade was wide, but rarely exceeded 24in (60cm) in length. Later, it was lengthened to 30in (75cm) because the cavalry needed an effective cutting weapon that could be used from horseback. The grip was remarkably uncomplicated. There was virtually no hand guard, although a rounded pommel afforded an easy grasp in battle. The strength of the gladius lay more in its function in conjunction with other equipment and Roman military tactics. In battle, the typical Roman tactic was to launch pila (javelins), followed by a charge of legionaries brandishing their gladii.

Most true collectors would give almost anything to possess a Roman gladius, but few examples of it have survived. As a sword, the gladius is perhaps the single most important type in human history, embodying artistic, historic, and geo-political factors unlike any other weapon. It is almost certainly the most difficult sword to collect.

Katzbalger

The Katzbalger was the standard broadsword in use in Germany and Central Europe at the beginning of the fifteenth century. It continued to dominate the battlefield for centuries thereafter.

The name may have derived from the German word *Katzbalger*, meaning an undisciplined tussle at close quarters. In some parts of Europe, it is also known as the landesknecht sword. Its blade was broad, straight, and double-edged, the grip was heavy, and the pommel, wide, often flaring to afford an excellent grip. Katzbalgers were often carried in a shoulder sling.

The oldest authentic example on display dates from 1515, and may be seen in Vienna, Austria.

Left **Roman tombstone found at Gloucester, United Kingdom, depicts a Roman cavalryman defeating an enemy soldier who wields a gladius (tombstone held by Gloucester City Museum).**

Kilij

In essence, a kilij is a Turkish saber, dating back to the rise of the Seljuk Turks, who, in 1055, established an empire in Asia Minor.

The kilij's blade is quite different from blades seen elsewhere in the Muslim world. It was broader, shorter, and less curved and could therefore be used for thrusting; although it seems to have been ineffective when used in this way. The kilij was almost wholly used as a cutting blade. The hilt, which resembled a pistol grip, was made of horn, ivory, or even of semiprecious stone, and only a slim crossbar protected the hand. The kilij was never anything but a combat weapon, and any inscriptions are of a suitably warlike nature. Because of its modest curve, the scabbard was hung in front, to allow the sword to be unsheathed quickly. Although it is the earliest Turkish weapon to be identified, the kilij was so effective that its design and blade length remained unchanged.

Kilijs are still made in some areas of Turkey, although price and availability are difficult to predict.

Rapier

Although always more ornamental than useful, the rapier could be deadly in the hands of an expert. At a time when the broadsword became the standard military weapon throughout Europe, the rapier developed into the customary sword for civilians of social standing. Essentially thrusting weapons, rapiers seem to have appeared first in Spain, spreading to the British Isles only in the sixteenth century. Nevertheless, it was in England that rapiers achieved their greatest popularity as social accoutrements.

Below **Spanish cup-hilt rapier with a Toledo blade, late seventeenth century. This type of hilt offered heavy protection for the hand.**

At first, rapiers were deemed suitable only for use as offensive weapons, although contemporary accounts suggest that they were effective against nothing more hazardous than the odd highwayman. It was nonetheless discovered that, wielded properly, a rapier could inflict serious damage. Yet, the rapier seems to have fallen from use even before it achieved the zenith of its popularity. In the seventeenth century, longer and heavier blades evolved, and the rapier was replaced by the smallsword, a more functional weapon.

Rapiers seem to be amongst the most easily found weapons of recent centuries. They are also the most lavishly decorated, which is why they are popular with collectors.

Below **A French gentleman's rapier (c1635–40), a very light weapon that would not have been very useful against a sturdier blade.**

Saber

The saber is a sword with a single edge and a slightly curved blade. It was the customary weapon of almost every country's cavalry throughout the eighteenth and nineteenth centuries. It was intended mainly as a cutting tool, especially effective when wielded by cavalrymen to inflict serious injuries to the heads and necks of ground troops. Sabers could also be used by dismounted riders for thrusting, when it would effectively skewer opponents.

The saber is probably the easiest of the major swords to collect. The standard armament of cavalrymen for several centuries, sabers continued to be made until comparatively recently. They are also comparatively inexpensive. A collection of sabers is a most attractive proposition for most edged-weapon enthusiasts.

Right **This chiseled and gilt saber was possibly made for Henri II of France (c1550) by the Italian swordsmith, Daniel Serravalo of Milan.**

Right **Craftsmanship and fighting efficiency combine in this selection of early nineteenth century European sabers.**
Left to Right **A rare example for a trooper of the Mounted Grenadiers of the Imperial Guard, c1800; a saber for a senior officer, possibly Imperial Guard, c1805; note the unusual grip, fashioned with mother-of-pearl scales, on this field officer's saber, c1800; dated 1820, this example, encased in a black leather scabbard with gilt mounts, would have been worn by a senior officer.**

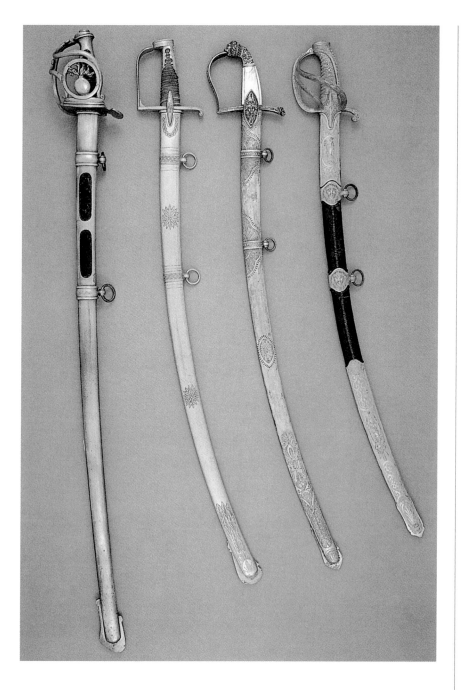

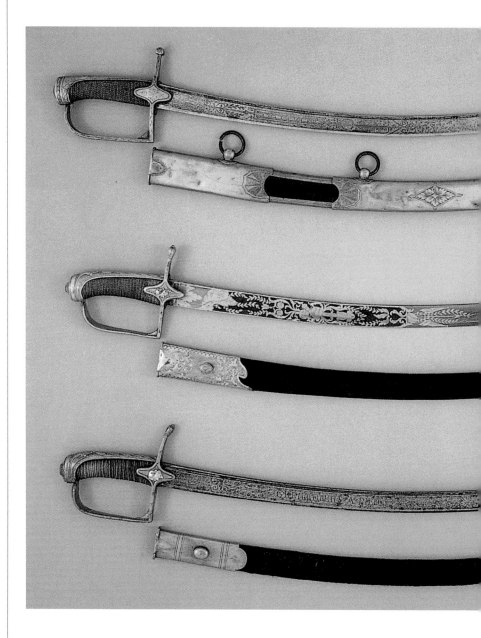

Left (Top to bottom) Foot
Grenadiers of the Imperial
Guard, c1805; Infantry of
the Imperial Guard, c1810;
Chasseurs à Cheval of the
Imperial Guard, c1810.

Scimitar

The scimitar is often considered to be the archetypal weapon of Islamic soldiers. In reality, however, it was originally a hunting sword, neither Turkish nor Arabic in provenance. It was once the shamshir ("lion's tail"), a Persian sword, whose design drifted east into India and west into Turkey.

Over the years, the scimitar evolved into the saber borne by the Persian cavalry. It had the pistol-style grip common to Islamic weapons, but, because of the extreme curvature of its narrow blade, the weapon was effective only for cutting. Although the curvature of the blade was pronounced, it was even and therefore easy to remove from its scabbard. Scabbards for scimitars usually had a spring that snapped open, facilitating the process of drawing the weapon.

The scimitar was the ultimate example of utility in warfare. Despite its lack of ornamentation — or perhaps because of it — many authorities regard the scimitar as the finest, most beautifully proportioned sword ever manufactured.

Below Indian scimitar, the hilt and mounts of enameled silver depicting fish (the symbol of the reigning house of Lucknow); late eighteenth century.

Far Right Indian late eighteenth century scimitar with a richly enameled silver hilt, and a fine Persian blade dating from the seventeenth century.

Smallswords

Smallswords were the direct descendants of the rapier. First seen at the end of the seventeenth century, they continued to be the standard sword for civilians for as long as edged weapons were carried. Designed solely for thrusting, the smallsword shared another characteristic with the rapier: its light construction and the difficulty in using it properly made the smallsword one of the least hazardous weapons ever used. It appears that, no matter how enthusiastically wielded in a fight, the smallsword inflicted permanent injury on very few people.

Smallswords are available to today's collectors. Though it is often difficult to tell precisely from descriptions in auction house catalogs, it is likely that a majority of the long-bladed weapons on sale are versions of the civilian smallsword.

Right For centuries, both the Spanish Navy and Army favored a type of smallsword that was referred to by the name "broadsword." The one depicted here stems from c1700.

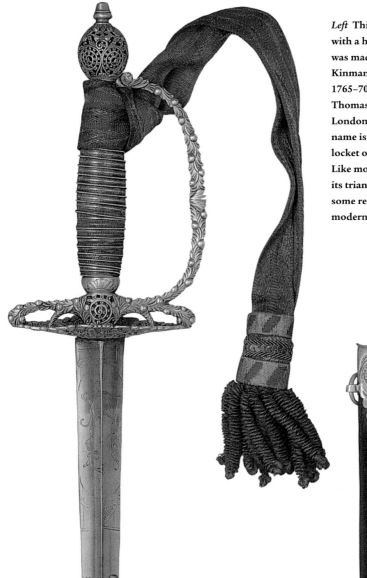

Left This smallsword, with a hilt of silver gilt, was made by William Kinman during 1765–70, and retailed by Thomas Dealtry (a London cutler), whose name is engraved on the locket of the scabbard. Like most smallswords, its triangular blade bears some resemblance to a modern bayonet.

Two-Handed Sword

Most people think of the medieval broadsword when they hear the expression "two-handed sword." The expression actually refers to any weapon large or heavy enough to require the use of both hands for effective wielding. These swords were generally used to direct overhead blows, but because they were so bulky, it was almost impossible to strike any but the least nimble assailants.

The Swiss used two-handed swords almost exclusively until the end of the fifteenth century, when it was officially suppressed. Interestingly, it was only at this time that they earned a reputation as the best mercenary soldiers in Europe. In the sixteenth century, the two-handed sword was the preferred choice for execution throughout most of Europe.

Two-handed swords were most widely used in the East. Neither Chinese nor Mongol hordes ever adopted the weapon, but the Japanese katana (fighting sword) is amongst the best known swords of this kind.

Below A German two-handed sword, c1540. This type of weapon is also known as a Katzbalger sword.

Right A two-handed sword, possibly English, c1450. Similar weapons have been excavated near the site of the battle of Castillon (1453), in France.

Below A two-handed sword (or "tuck") from Germany early sixteenth century. A light weapon with a blade of 41in (104cm).

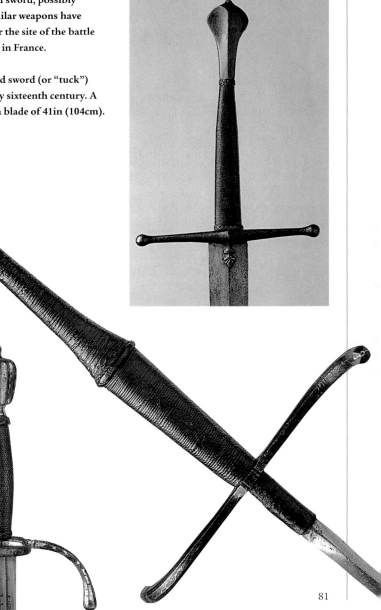

Cutlass

The cutlass still enjoys an aura of mystique and adventure, largely due to its association with literary fiction and cinema.

During the late eighteenth and early nineteenth centuries, naval fighting swords became increasingly ineffective for battle. By 1812, American sailors started using blades with a pronounced curve. These weapons were firmly based on the cavalry saber, but were distinctively designed for use at sea. The swords were lavishly decorated with heavily embellished hilts, the size was reduced to a manageable length, and the hilt was proportionately shortened. These swords closely resembled the Persian scimitar.

In 1859, the United States Marine Corps was ordered to abandon these glamorous weapons, and to adopt a new naval weapon. Officially, this had to have a blade of approximately 26–29in (66–74cm) long. The cutlass was prescribed for enlisted men, who never wore it unless forced to. However, it proved to be popular with officers.

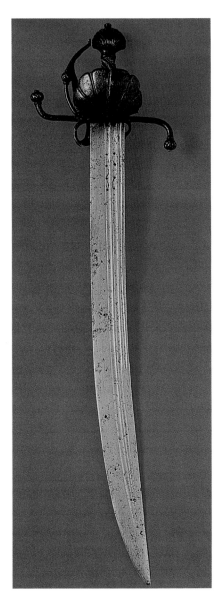

Right "Dusägge" German short sword or cutlass, c1580–90. These weapons seem to have been used by military and civilians alike.

In 1790, a weapon designated as a cutlass was issued in limited numbers in the Royal Navy. The blade was long and slender with a sturdy flat edge, but the cutting edge was less than ideal. The hand guard at the shoulder was wider and stronger than earlier swords, while the knuckle guard almost rolled back on itself from the pommel to the hand guard, so that it was virtually impossible to lose hold of the weapon.

The first regulation cutlass was ordered for the Royal Navy in 1798, but it enjoyed little success. Although clearly unsatisfactory in many ways, the Admiralty, amongst others, still encouraged manufacturers to produce it. At the time, Britain was involved in the Napoleonic Wars and needed thousands of weapons. In 1814, the Board of Ordinance recognized that improvements were needed in the cutlass. This time the blade had a pronounced but smooth curve from the mount to the tip. The length and the hilt were standardized, and the knuckle guard was no longer oval, flaring widely in a pear shape to protect the hand.

It is ironic that the ideal weapon for hand-to-hand sea combat was developed at the end of that era, and long after the pirates with whom we so readily associate it.

Fighting Sword

By 1770, the naval sword transformed into what is called the fighting sword. The first fighting swords were straight and single-edged, but by the outbreak of the American War of Independence in 1776, the cutting edge acquired a slight curve. Knuckle guards became elaborate, those of Royal Navy swords often displaying the fouled anchor or lion's head motifs. Blades became shorter, making it possible to inflict more damage. By the time the War of Independence ended in 1783, fighting swords were heavily decorated.

In 1796, the British Army adopted a standardized sword for its officers. This was based on the Prussian infantry sword that had been carried by the forces of Frederick the Great in the 1740s. The cross guard became heavier and pommels were elaborately decorated. The British Navy followed the Army's lead and, despite its size, this weapon which was always known as the infantry officer's sword, enjoyed a vogue well into the nineteenth century. For the first time, patriotic inscriptions such as "for King and Country" were added, and the hilts were lavishly decorated with maritime motifs. Even among naval officers, however, it was always regarded more as a ceremonial weapon than a fighting implement.

In America and Germany, the French version of the fighting sword achieved acceptance. It was strikingly different from the British version. The hilts were usually more flamboyant, and tended to slant forward, which was believed to provide a better grasp and increase the impact of the blows delivered. This style remained popular until the middle of the nineteenth century.

Hanger

The first distinctly recognizable blade was the hanger, so named because it hung from the belt of the wearer. The original hanger was a cheap weapon. It was given little attention in production, and, if scabbards existed, they were roughly crafted leather sheaths.

The swords themselves were straightforward and rather flimsy looking. The mounts were usually gilt, brass or silver, because of the metals' ability to resist corrosion. Hangers were often decorated with naval motifs; scallop shells were popular, and in some parts of the Caribbean the sword was colloquially called "the shell."

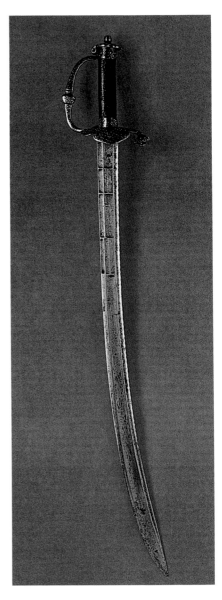

Right **Single-edged English silver encrusted hunting hanger (riding sword), c1640–1650. The fine blade was probably imported from Germany.**

As long ago as 1684, Esquemeling, a London-based writer specializing in tales of piracy and bloodshed, illustrated his books with drawings that showed hangers being used by both pirates and law enforcers. This is, without doubt, the weapon with which buccaneers were familiar.

Hangers have been occasionally found by divers off old pirate strongholds in the Caribbean. Several old weapons were recovered in 1986 from the pirate vessel, the *Whyday*.

Naval Saber

By 1800, British fighting swords were beginning to acquire curved blades, which seem to have been first made by swordmakers in Birmingham. Hilts were reduced in length and, although knuckle guards were retained and the grips were made of ivory or a similar substance, the swords became less elaborate.

Eventually, the blades became increasingly curved and shortened to just under 30in (75cm). These swords are known as naval sabers.

Spadroon

This curious weapon was first seen in the 1780s. It is sometimes called the infantry officer's sword of 1786, but this is, in fact, a misnomer. The spadroon was intended to provide both cut and thrust, but it

was less than successful. The blades, at 30–32in (75–82cm), were too long, as effective thrusting blades must be straight, rigid, and relatively compact.

Although a British invention, the spadroon was adopted in Scandinavia, Germany, and in parts of America. It was never popular in France, where it was known by the derogatory name of the *épée anglais*. The spadroon quickly vanished from naval arsenals. It probably lasted the longest in the United States Army, where it was still a recommended weapon for infantry officers as late as 1821.

Below **Shown here is the detail of the single-edged English silver-encrusted hunting hanger.**

Hunting Sword

By 1700, the hanger had transformed into the hunting sword. The hunting sword had a shorter and more curvaceous blade than its predecessor, although the hilt remained a standard 6in (15cm). The hunting sword was popularized in Britain by Admiral John Benbow (1653–1702). He ran away to sea as a boy and joined the Merchant Marine. From 1689, he served in the Royal Navy. A popular hero in Britain, he was celebrated in Robert Louis Stevenson's *Treasure Island*.

The French version of the sword was widely used on the other side of the Atlantic, where American sailors preferred the more elaborate style, with longer blades and hilts, and the overall length often being as much as 24in (60cm). The swords were often embossed with silver, and the scabbards were ornate. The handles tended to be flared, widening toward the pommel.

Right A hunting sword with etched and gilt single-edged blade by Ambrosius Gemlich of Munich (c1540). The gilt bronze hilt dates from the seventeenth century.

Above Hunting sword and sheath;
the silver hilt is cast, and chased with a design
showing an American Indian fighting two
mountain lions. Emperor Napoleon III gifted
this to his friend and fellow collector, the
fourth Marquess of Hertford, in about 1860.

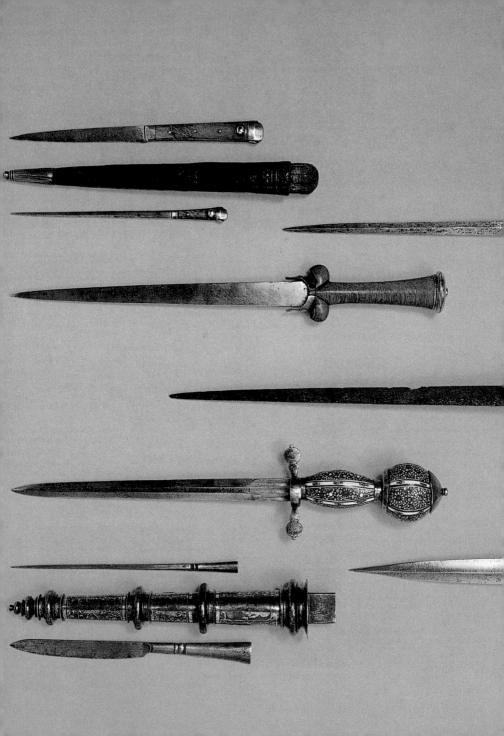

Daggers and Knives

History of Daggers and Knives

A knife is any edge tool used as a cutting instrument that has a pointed blade with a sharp edge and a handle. A dagger is a short knife with a pointed blade used for piercing or stabbing.

The oldest crafted weapon was not, in fact, the sword, but the knife. These small edged cutting tools were hammered, chiseled, and formed out of almost any substance. Such implements were certainly used half a million years ago, primarily for cutting meat, scraping hides, or shaping wooden implements. The Stone Age was almost over before what might be termed a "fighting knife" appeared.

Ironically, stone knives may have been widely used even after metal weapons were developed. Some beautiful ones were crafted in ancient Egypt, Africa, and Scandinavia. In fact, Egyptian pieces are amongst the oldest stone examples in existence. In Europe, most stone knives were made in Scandinavia. In fact, so widespread was the use of stone daggers in Scandinavia that archaeologists refer to the period 1800–500 BCE as the Dolktid Period (Dagger Period). The earliest Scandinavian blades were almost diamond-like in shape, with one of the long ends somewhat flattened to ensure a better fit with the hilt.

Not all stone knives are ancient. In the Americas, where the common stone was obsidian, the Aztecs made attractive and ornate blades of dark green or black. As recently as a century ago, Native Americans made dozens of obsidian blades everyday. The fracture of obsidian is extremely conchoidal — skilled artisans held the stone between their feet and simply broke off sharp-edged flakes.

Despite widespread use, such stone implements have always suffered from one major drawback: although relatively sharp edges could be achieved, once chipped or broken they could not be repaired or resharpened. The development of copper-working remedied this situation to an extent, but copper blades had to be very thick or wide for such a malleable metal to withstand any real impact. At most, a serviceable blade was limited to being no longer than 6in (15cm).

To overcome this problem, blades were initially made parallel for most of their length from the handle before tapering to a point. This was an improvement, but still not sufficient to provide long-lasting weapons. Attempts to make longer copper weapons with the tang as a single piece made them more prone to snap on impact. The addition of a central rib made the blade stronger but it was only the discovery of bronze that allowed for the production of durable blades. Metal hilts were also made with grips fashioned from ivory, bone, and even pearl.

Right Union soldiers carried side knives as well as swords. These were supposedly standardized, though there were several versions in existence. Like their Confederate counterparts, these Union knives were hardly ever employed in actual battle.

Left An Italian cinquedea, a short sword for civilian wear (c1500), with it's original *cuir bouilli* (hardened leather) sheath.

The technology of the Bronze Age gradually reached across Europe along the trade routes of the rivers Danube and Elbe, and bronze daggers from the Dolktid Period have been found as far north as Scandinavia. Weapons dating from this period were not intended to be works of art. Grips were cylindrical and pommels were flat and plain. By 1400 BCE, knives were being cast as a single unit in northern Italy, the Rhone valley in France, and central Germany. When not cast as a solid piece with the blade, the handle was usually riveted. Half a dozen small rivets were usually sufficient, although some Bronze Age pieces from southern England have as many as 32 rivets.

Among the finds at Hallstatt in upper Austria, which are thought to represent the transitional period between the Bronze and Iron Ages, were knives of bronze overlaid with gold, some even with gold-leaf decoration on knife and scabbard.

Single-edged blades recovered in France from around 500 BCE, reveal that knives had fallen from favor. For almost a thousand years the dagger was more or less consigned to oblivion. The Roman war machine relied on the gladius and even senior commanders spurned the dagger for ceremonial purposes. It was not until the victorious Charlemagne instituted the *hari bannus* (the hereban) that daggers made a comeback. He made military service a condition of owning more than a pittance of property, and thereby founded martial morale on the defense and extension of one's land. Every freeman, at the call to arms, had to report in full equipment to the local count. The Frankish counts were the lieutenants of administrative districts, and in their role as *bannus* were responsible for the military fitness of their constituents. Within each district, groups of men were made responsible for providing each soldier with a sword, shield, spear, and dagger.

This group of edged weapons — whether used for fighting, self-defense, or simply murder — is one of the largest, and the most distinctive and important are examined here.

Left and Below **Details showing the provenance carved on knife handles. The one left belonged to a member of the 3rd Maryland Artillery, whilst the one below began life in Tennessee in 1864.**

Types of Daggers

Many types of dagger have been developed, their names usually referring to the look or the style of fighting they were associated with, for example the ear dagger, quillon dagger, main gauche (*left-hand*), and stiletto.

Cinquedea

In the late fifthteenth century, smiths at the Villa Basilica in northern Italy designed a weapon that closely resembled a small sword. This was the cinquedea, a dagger that derived its name from the fact that its savage blade, which was somewhat like a garden trowel, was five fingers wide at the shoulder.

Original cinquedeas are extremely rare, and many fakes were produced, especially in the 1840s. Equally rare are examples of their original scabbards, which were elaborately decorated, leading one London museum to describe them as "the finest pieces of art in leather known."

Far Right Italian cinquedea, a dagger or short sword for civilian wear, c1500. The wide and sweeping quillons were decorated with motifs taken from popular mythology.

Right The cinquedea was carried horizontally across the buttocks so that it could be drawn with the left hand from the back or belt. This example, dating from c1480, probably comes from Ferrara, Italy.

Left-Hand Dagger

Despite its name, the left-hand dagger was not a weapon specifically made for left-handed use alone. It was a companion piece for the rapier, and for years, to defend with the rapier and to strike with the left-hand dagger was a well-used manoeuver.

The left-hand dagger was usually made as a pair with the sword, and the two have been widely described as "the only right and true gentlemanly weapons." The dagger had a stiff, straight blade, and was usually as gaudily decorated as the rapier, especially around the knuckle guard. The two weapons were popular from the early sixteenth until the late seventeenth century, and in Spain they continued to be used until the eighteenth century.

Left A "Spanish" left-hand dagger (*main gauche*) for use with a cup-hilt rapier. Possibly Italian (Neopolitan), made under Spanish influence in the third quarter of the seventeenth century.

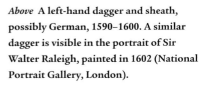

Above A left-hand dagger and sheath, possibly German, 1590–1600. A similar dagger is visible in the portrait of Sir Walter Raleigh, painted in 1602 (National Portrait Gallery, London).

Rondel Dagger

The rondel dagger originated during the first half of the fifteenth century. Named for its disk-shaped pommel and guard, it was primarily used in southern Europe. The pommel was formed of two solid disks of wood, and a long tang, which was riveted to form the grip that ran through the blocks.

In the fourteenth century, an interesting version of the rondel appeared. This was the eared dagger, which shares its heritage with the blade known to the Turks as the *yataghan* and to the Cossacks as the *shashqa*. The pommel of eared daggers was split in two, which often resembled badly formed images of Mickey Mouse. The design allowed the thumb to be hooked over the pommel, in order to impart greater force to the stabbing blow.

Despite its appearance, the eared dagger became widely associated with royalty and yet was also a favorite weapon with assassins in Italy during the fifteenth and sixteenth centuries.

Below Left **A rondel dagger, possibly French, from c1450. Similar brass studs have been found on a rondel dagger recovered from the Thames.**

Below Right **Rondel or "ear" dagger, Venetian or Spanish, dating from c1500. It would have been held point downward, with the thumb lying over the top of the grip, between the "ears."**

Quillon

The quillon, which is simply a small version of a sword, can be traced back to the Hallstatt culture, the Celtic civilization that represented the transition between the Bronze and Iron Ages. The blades taper evenly, the pommels are round or crescent-shaped, and the crossguards are solid.

The dagger appeared in its present form in the thirteenth century. Primarily a knightly weapon, the quillon was worn suspended from the belt by a ring through the pommel; this gave rise to its alternative name, the ring dagger. Like the knightly class with which it was associated, the quillon fell from favor by 1500.

Quillons still exist in private collections in central Europe, yet because of their association with knights, are expensive.

Right **Stiletto, made entirely of chiseled steel; Italian (Brescian), dating from c1650.**

Far Right **Stiletto, probably West European, dating from the early seventeenth century.**

Stiletto

The weapon known as the stiletto first gained popularity in the sixteenth century, and remained in favor for about 150 years. It was a smaller version of the *stilo* (Italian dagger), and the stiletto's stiff blade, somewhat triangular in cross-section, made it useful only when used with a stabbing motion. The hilt was usually steel, with a simple crossguard.

Stilettos became widely accepted in southern Europe when edicts forbidding weapons to be carried were passed; the slim daggers could

be easily hidden in clothing. They could also be hidden inside hollow staffs, known as brandestocs, a practice that was widespread in Europe. Stilettos were also often carried by artillery troops because the scales for measuring powder charges were engraved on the scabbards.

Although it was not an especially effective weapon, the stiletto was made in all shapes and sizes and has acquired a reputation for being used for murder and assassination.

Swiss Dagger

The Swiss dagger is sometimes confused with the schweizerdegen (the Swiss short sword), and it is a truly large and brutal-looking weapon. It is also called the holbein, after the painter Hans Holbein the younger, who produced wood engravings entitled *The Dance of Death*, motifs from which were frequently engraved on Swiss daggers. The daggers were usually flamboyantly decorated, and the scabbards were festooned with designs depicting scenes from folklore. The Swiss dagger is the prototype of the German SS dagger, which was first issued in 1936. Many of these were highly decorated, and scabbards were often inscribed with the SS motto *Meine Ehre Heisst Treue* (My Honor is Loyalty).

In their original form, Swiss daggers are extremely difficult to acquire. Similar weapons are obtainable, however, as are the SS daggers.

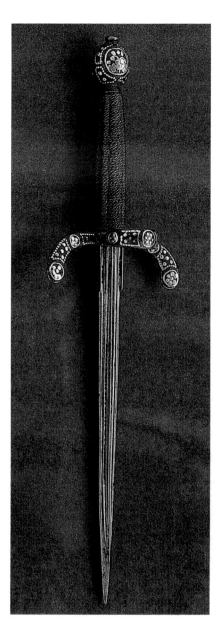

Right **Swiss dagger (possibly German) dating from c1600, with encrusted silver decoration.**

Below The gilt-copper
sheath of the Swiss dagger
depicts the Legend of
Virginia, with Appius
Claudius III on the
Judgement Seat.

Left Swiss dagger or
holbein, c1560. The dagger
itself, though stylistically
correct, is a nineteenth
century replacement.

Daggers of the Third Reich

No discussion of daggers would be complete without reference to the edged weapons produced during the Third Reich. Most of these weapons were purely ceremonial, and were produced as a sop to Hitler's passion for the trappings of the Reich. Swords, for example, were commonly borne on dress occasions, although they were never seriously considered to have any military value.

Daggers, however, were another matter. They played a prominent part in the riots that brought Hitler to power in 1933, and the SS (schutzstaffel) knives, first issued in 1936, were efficient weapons,

Far Left **The German Army's all-purpose knife was also a dagger — and a fine weapon. However, they were never regarded as very useful in combat, and were therefore most often employed for a variety of non-combat functions.**

Left **The Nazi Luftwaffe dagger was issued in large numbers to German paratroopers in World War II.**

Right **German World War II daggers were allotted on the basis of service and rank. Here we see a 1937 pattern Luftwaffe dagger in the context of an Oberleutnant's uniform and other memorabilia.**

intricately decorated with silver handles and ivory inlays.

Despite the popularity of Nazi weapons, it is still not difficult to acquire blades from that era, especially some of the smaller types. However, there is a view that these weapons are overpriced, and even though building a modest collection would not be impossible, there is always the possibility that the allure of the Third Reich weapons will, in time, pass from fashion.

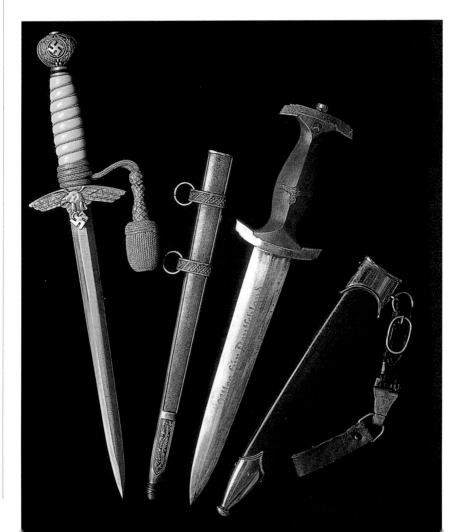

Baselard

One of the most popular daggers was the baselard. It is believed to have been so named because it was invented in Basle, Switzerland.

Right **The baselard is traditionally Swiss in origin. This example dates from c1530.**

The baselard is the forerunner of the Swiss dagger, first appearing at the end of the thirteenth century. It was longer than most daggers – sometimes almost as long as a short sword. A simple but sturdy crosspiece, the weapon acquired its distinctive appearance from its pommel, which resembled the capital letter "I." The blades tapered evenly to a point, and the grips were made of two pieces of horn, wood, or ivory riveted together. Used by people in all walks of life, including knights, the baselard dagger can be collected even today.

Far Left **A Third Reich Luftwaffe dagger of the post-1937 era, an offshoot of the original 1936 SS dagger. The German paratroops and special commandos under Skorzeny were adept at employing these edged weapons – though theirs, however, were more functional and less grandiose.**

Left **This SSA dagger, based on an older Swiss model, was used extensively in the street battles which brought Hitler to power in January 1933.**

Types of Knives

Legend has it that in 1830, Colonel Jim Bowie of Kentucky visited a knifemaker named James Black in Arkansas. What transpired was the most famous blade in American history — the Bowie knife.

Bowie Knife

Bowie did not intend for his knife to be used for fighting. Yet it was used in more murders and duels in American history than any other weapon, besides the pistol. The knife is single-edged, with a straight, powerful back, a sharp point, and a blade curving gently to meet it. By the middle of the nineteenth century, the Bowie knife's fame spread, and a number of companies were manufacturing it. Ultimately, more Bowie knives were manufactured in Britain than in the United States.

Today, the Bowie knife is regarded as the quintessential American weapon. However, many fakes have been made over the years, and collectors should only purchase examples that bear the name of the original owner, which was engraved on the handle or shoulder of the blade until the nineteenth century.

Hauswehren

Many edged weapons are associated with members of the knightly class or nobility, but peasants, too, were armed. In almost every European country, the hauswehren knife was commonly used by peasants to protect themselves and their homes.

Some writers have suggested that hauswehren knives are derived from the Viking scramasax, while others have propounded the less likely theory that they are the forerunner of the Bowie knife. Although they were simple, hauswehren knives should not be thought of as ordinary — they closely resembled butcher's knives, and although officially regarded as working knives, they could also be used as effective weapons.

Right **A stylized painting of Jim Bowie at the Alamo, wearing his famed "Arkansas toothpick." The character shown does resemble the frontiersman, judging from other known portraits of Bowie.**

Commando Knife

The commando, or combat, knife is not usually included in discussions of edged weapons, with more attention being lavished on costlier and more exotic models. A combat knife is, strictly, a weapon designed to be used as a side arm; it is not an all-purpose tool. Cutting implements such as pangas, bolos, and machetes are not fighting knives.

The best-known examples are currently out of vogue. In World War I, the trench knife was most widely used; it was double-edged, and had a set of brass knuckles as a hand guard. However, it is too bulky and awkward to gain acceptance in modern times. In World War II, the best-known weapon was the British-made, Fairbairn-Sykes commando knife, a variant of which was popular with American Marines in the Pacific. Unfortunately, this weapon proved to be too brittle to survive, its use being limited to opening letters or taking the tops off bottles of beer. Today, there are two main types of commando knife. One is broad, flat, and double-edged; the other resembles a stiletto.

Building up a collection of combat knives may prove to be one of the easiest types of collection to amass. Any military surplus store houses examples, and some stores specialize in them, although acquiring antiques may prove difficult.

Above The trench knife's brass knuckle configuration added to its value in hand-to-hand combat during World War I. These two examples date from 1917–1918.

Above Before the advent of cheap, durable scissors, this 1904 American hospital corps knife would have been used for a range of functions.

Above A selection of utility and combat knives, employed by American and British forces since 1939.

Above The machete could be a very efficient weapon, and was useful for all sorts of functions in thick terrain. However, it was never really deemed to be a fighting knife.

Navaja

Some time during the fifteenth century, cutlers hailing from several cities in Spain crafted the navaja. The forerunner of the switchblade knife (flick-knife), the navaja featured a slightly oval blade that folded into the handle.

The first manual to discuss fighting with knives mentions the navaja. It was written in 1849 by someone known only as M. d. R., probably a disinherited Italian or Spanish aristocrat. The manual was aimed at the working classes, and the author made frequent derogatory comments about the "so-called decent classes" and named knifefighters *barateros*. The navaja was generally employed to slash at an opponent, but M. d. R. wrote that any tactic that gained the advantage was acceptable. "If all else failed," he wrote, "throw the knife at your opponent to give yourself time to escape through the window."

Versions of the navaja are still in use throughout the Spanish-speaking world, and a persistent collector could acquire a considerable number. Although it would not be possible to establish an historic provenance for each weapon, they would form a fascinating group.

Scramasax

The scramasax was the knife used by the Vikings of Scandinavia who raided and settled around the coasts of Britain and Western Europe during the eighth and tenth centuries. Although the knife did not originate in Scandinavia, it was the Vikings who made it their own. Scholars believe the word *sax* refers to "sword," and that *scrama* means "a wound-making implement;" the word, therefore, translates tautologically as "wound-making sword."

The scramasax has, in a masterpiece of understatement, been described as a sturdy knife. The blades were anything from 4in to 20in (10cm to 50cm) long, but all were single-edged and triangular in cross-section. The handles were broad and riveted just below the pommel, which was round or onion-shaped, and the grips were made of leather or wood.

The scramasax remained popular across Europe for several centuries and was used in Scandinavia until the twelfth century, while its variant was carried in England as late as the fifteenth century. The scramasax therefore represents a transition between Iron Age daggers and more sophisticated fighting knives with which we are familiar today.

Dirk

One of the most misunderstood of fighting knives is the dirk. Its immediate forerunner was the Scottish ballock knife, which was widely used by the 14th century but dates back to 1050 if not before.

By the 17th century a longer bladed knife than the ballock knife appeared and in 1650 this was universally known as a "durk." The knife's origins are obscure, but the spelling that is now current was apparently the result of an erroneous entry by Dr Johnson in his dictionary in 1755. By 1700 blades were about 15in (38cm) long – as long as a small sword. By the middle of the century the dirk was elaborate. The grips were wrapped in silver wire, the pommels were dome-shaped, and the blades had broadened shoulders, known as haunches. Scabbards were generally simple, although the more complex ones had exterior pockets to carry eating utensils and extra knives called "by knyfs."

The Jacobite rebellions of 1715 and 1745 led to the passing of several Disarming Acts, designed to outlaw the dirk. They had the opposite effect, and dirks proliferated. In many ways, the dirk is still the national blade of Scotland, although it developed independently elsewhere.

Right A Scottish dirk, sheath, and belt: the blades of both the dirk and its by-knife are struck MOYES for John Moyes, a cutler working in Edinburgh between 1793 and 1824.

Below This is a good example of a World War I implement combining a Mark III weapon and Mark II scabbard. It was evidently first issued to a member of the Highland Pipers and Drummers.

Naval Dirk

Full-length swords were not the only type of blade found upon the water, but naval dirks are often overlooked in discussions of naval edged weapons. These elongated, elaborate knives first appeared among naval officers at the time of the American War of Independence (1776–83). Originally, many may have been made from broken swords, which could be cut off and new points shaped. The scabbards could also be cut down to accommodate the new weapons. They were unofficial and optional, although in the nineteenth century they were adopted by naval midshipmen on both sides of the Atlantic as something of a regular accoutrement.

A gradual tradition developed, especially in the English-speaking navies, of wearing a companion blade to the longer sword. This was a popular trend for many years, and naval dirks began to be manufactured to serve this very purpose. Some American dirks exactly reflect the decorations on the companion pieces.

Naval dirks had blades 12–14in (30–36cm) in length and hilts 3½–5½in (9–14cm) in length, although the size of the handle was not as important as the length of the blade. These weapons were only used in close attack, so there was little need to achieve a fine balance between the mount and blade.

The dirk gained official recognition in the Royal Navy c1800. A blade with a cutting edge some

Above **This shows a cavalry sabre that has been cut down to a knife, c1872. Over time many swords have been converted in a similar way. It was probably the inspiration for the original naval dirk.**

Right A Royal Navy midshipman's dirk
dating from Victorian times, whose lion's
head motif was standard for British objects
of the era. The dirk was generally disdained
by senior officers, and became the symbol
of the midshipman.

1in (41cm) in length was produced by
Tatham and Egg. This weapon was
intended as a symbol of rank, and it
was regarded as something of a joke
by senior commanders. It became
standard among midshipmen.

In the United States the curved
dirk became popular some years
before it was accepted in Britain,
although it does seem that the Royal
Navy long recognized its value as a
miniature cutlass. These weapons
tended to have longer blades —
15–16in (38–40cm) — but,
because of the curve, they were not
cumbersome. The hilts gradually
became rather over-decorated. In
Britain the dirk attained its greatest
popularity during the Regency of
1811–20. By c1810 both it and its
scabbard were encrusted with gilt
and other decorations, including the
lion's head motif. American dirks of
the same period bore the eagle's head.

A major question that arises in any
consideration of the naval dirk is:
why were they worn? It would appear
that in the Royal Navy, at least, they
were actually seen as fighting
implements, although they can hardly
have been effective when longer and
more efficient weapons were used.
Americans seem to have regarded
them as a more convenient way of
distinguishing officers while aboard
ship than a cumbersome full-length
sword. But in the face of danger, they
were quickly abandoned in favor of
more powerful blades.

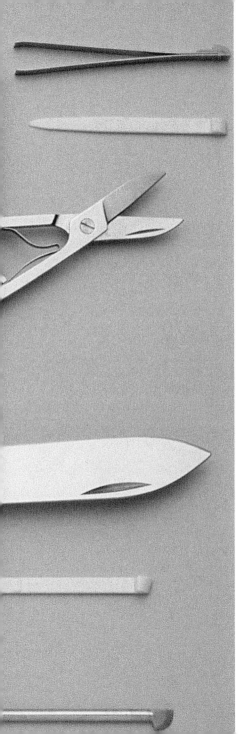

Pocketknives

Pocketknives

At first glance pocketknives seem such an everyday item, it is a wonder why so many people collect them. Yet it is precisely their familiar charm and infinite variety that gives them their appeal.

As tool-using creatures *par excellence*, we are always sure to have our trusty pocketknife with us! But a pocketknife is more than just a tool — it is a mechanical device, a work of great craft and technology, and even an elaborate work of art. To the affluent and sophisticated, fine pocketknives are like personal jewelry, and collecting them has been an enjoyable habit for many centuries. In 1862, Abraham Lincoln was presented with a handsome five-blade knife, which recently sold at an auction for nearly 100,000USD!

Today, there are many exclusive shops around the world that sell exquisite handcrafted folding knives, some of them engraved by the world's leading engravers, and at prices that range from several hundred US dollars up to 50,000USD each — quite a sum for an everyday item!

Beyond these technical, esthetic, and status considerations, a pocketknife of any age is a historical artifact, made at a particular time and place, and for a specific market. Because pocketknives are universal items that have been around since ancient times, their various forms, usages, styles, and brands have proliferated beyond imagination — efforts to document and classify them have occasionally approached

Left **Roman folding knife handle (base missing), depicting an embracing couple in bronze.**

the complexity of a paleontologist's work. Less than half have been documented, and old brands are being rediscovered everyday.

This section intends to serve as a basic introduction to pocketknives, and as such, assumes no prior knowledge on the part of the reader. Nevertheless, it contains a wealth of information that will prove valuable and revealing to the most advanced of collectors, knife dealers, and

manufacturers in the cutlery industry. More specifically, this section caters to the collector or enthusiastic pocketknife fan, to explain why certain knives are interesting and collectible, and therefore, valuable. With study and experience, one can learn to read these artifacts as precisely as an archeologist reads potsherds, and thus enhance your enjoyment of pocketknife collecting.

Below **Case XX Made in the United States 5-dot (1975) premium penknife, red-bone handles.**

Origin and Evolution

The story of pocketknives prior to the eighteenth century is part conjectural, part archeological. Excavations have revealed figural folding knives that date from the later years of the Roman Empire, which means that they were not exactly "pocket" knives, as sewn-on pockets were not yet invented!

Ancient and medieval folding knives made up for their technical deficiencies with an abundance of exuberant decoration. The earliest-known folding knives also had no back springs in their handles. The job of a pocketknife's spring is to apply tension to the blade and to keep it in place, when both open and closed. Without a spring, friction alone can keep a folding blade from flopping around. To this day, inexpensive folding knives are made in the ancient Roman style — without back springs. These are called penny knives, because the plainest versions of such knives used to be sold for a penny a piece.

The idea of the spring-back knife seems to be older, but reliable spring steel was a product of the mid-eighteenth century. It was the invention of Benjamin Huntsman, a clock-maker from Sheffield, England. Sheffield's cutlers soon learned to use Huntsman's crucible cast steel for blades and springs, and this new metal became the basis of the city's global preeminence as a cutlery center.

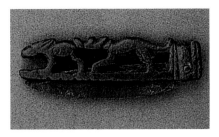

Above **Roman folding knife; the bronze openwork is half cast in the form of a hound catching a rabbit; second to fourth century CE.**

The generation after Huntsman's invention witnessed remarkable advances in cutlery design and technology. In Paris, France, the cheap and factory-produced pocketknife, or penny knife, was a notable eighteenth century development. Much of the basic design and technology of modern cutlery was created there at that time, largely by master cutler Jean-Jacques Perret. Perret set down a detailed record of his work in *The Art of the Cutler*, published in 1771; more than a century later, inventors the world over were still receiving patents for cutlery mechanisms that were copied from Perret's book.

Despite the advent of factory mass-production, high-quality folding knives were being made by hand until the mid-nineteenth century. To collectors, perhaps the most remarkable knives of that period were the folding side arms. Ornate and usually large, these folding dirks, bowie knives, and folding-knife-pistol combinations were made in infinite variation well into the early twentieth century, both for domestic sales and for export. As mass markets began to develop, standardization of pocketknife patterns for sale gradually advanced.

From the 1840s, emigrant cutlers from Europe began to develop a pocket cutlery industry in America, where resources were plentiful, but skilled labor was scarce. Manufacturers thus pioneered machine methods and simplified processes, another force that favored standardized patterns.

From the 1880s up to 1940, pocketknives evolved primarily through marketing and design. Technology was remarkably stable during that period, which is viewed by collectors today as the golden age of pocket cutlery. In 1914, the invention of stainless steel revolutionized table cutlery, but had no effect on the pocket cutlery industry until after 1950.

Left **A. G. Alford Sporting Goods, Baltimore, MD (late nineteenth century retailer), large horseman's knife, made in Sheffield, United Kingdom.**

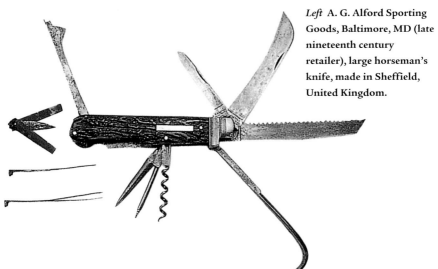

Making of Pocketknives

The journey of pocketknife-making has been a long and innovative one. The drawings opposite, from a catalog dating back to the 1900s, show how a typical, equal-end jackknife of the time was made.

The first step was to forge the blades from a carbon-steel strip (Nos. 1 and 2), usually a punch-press operation (as in the United States), or done by hand (as in Sheffield, England). The forged blades were then die-cut to shape and heat treated, after which the tangs were drilled, the surfaces ground, and the flats of the tang filed (Nos. 3 and 4). Springs were produced in much the same way as blades, except they were not forged before being die-cut (Nos. 5–7). The parts for the frame were made with chunks of nickel silver or mild steel. These were die-cut from thick stock, and then stamped or "coined" to form the bolsters, usually with a stud projecting from the inner surface (Nos. 9–11). Properly spaced holes were then drilled in strips of brass, with pairs of bolsters chopped on to these (Nos. 12 and 13). Then the strips were cut with pattern dies to make the final shape of the handle (No. 14). The resulting frame piece was called a "scale".

Meanwhile, the handle covers were prepared from wood, bone, ivory, pearly, stag, or synthetic materials (No. 15), and fitted to the scales, with the front cover being inletted to fit the shield (Nos. 16 and 17). Holes were drilled for rivets, and also one in each bolster, one in each end of the cover, two in the shield (No. 18), and one in the bottom center, to anchor the spring. The handle and shield rivets were then set, and the knife was assembled (No. 20) and given to a cutler, who did the final adjusting to ensure its smooth operation. Lastly, the blades were polished, honed, and etched (No. 21)

Above **Ka-Bar 1189 folding hunter, cutaway demonstrator model. Note internal music-wire spring.**

OAK LEAF POCKET KNIVES
HOW THEY ARE MADE

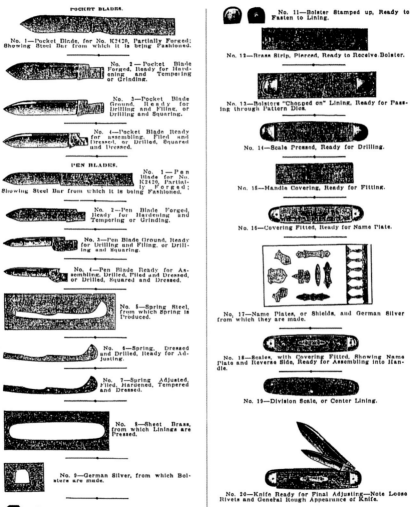

POCKET BLADES.

No. 1—Pocket Blade, for No. K2420, Partially Forged; Showing Steel Bar from which it is being Fashioned.

No. 2—Pocket Blade Forged, Ready for Hardening and Tempering or Grinding.

No. 3—Pocket Blade Ground, Ready for Drilling and Filing, or Drilling and Squaring.

No. 4—Pocket Blade Ready for assembling, Filed and Dressed, or Drilled, Squared and Dressed.

PEN BLADES.

No. 1—Pen Blade for No. K2420, Partially Forged; Showing Steel Bar from which it is being Fashioned.

No. 2—Pen Blade Forged, Ready for Hardening and Tempering or Grinding.

No. 3—Pen Blade Ground, Ready for Drilling and Filing, or Drilling and Squaring.

No. 4—Pen Blade Ready for Assembling, Drilled, Filed and Dressed, or Drilled, Squared and Dressed.

No. 5—Spring Steel, from which Spring is Produced.

No. 6—Spring, Dressed and Drilled, Ready for Adjusting.

No. 7—Spring Adjusted, Filed, Hardened, Tempered and Dressed.

No. 8—Sheet Brass, from which Linings are Pressed.

No. 9—German Silver, from which Bolsters are made.

No. 10—Blank for Bolster, Pressed Ready for Stamping.

No. 11—Bolster Stamped up, Ready to Fasten to Lining.

No. 12—Brass Strip, Pierced, Ready to Receive Bolster.

No. 13—Bolsters "Chopped on" Lining, Ready for Passing through Pattern Dies.

No. 14—Scale Pressed, Ready for Drilling.

No. 15—Handle Covering, Ready for Fitting.

No. 16—Covering Fitted, Ready for Name Plate.

No. 17—Name Plates, or Shields, and German Silver from which they are made.

No. 18—Scales, with Covering Fitted, Showing Name Plate and Reverse Side, Ready for Assembling into Handle.

No. 19—Division Scale, or Center Lining.

No. 20—Knife Ready for Final Adjusting—Note Loose Rivets and General Rough Appearance of Knife.

Factors and Factories

Originally, the word "factory" meant the warehouse of a factor. A factor was primarily a merchant who commissioned independent craftsmen or skilled laborers to produce his goods. In the knife trade, independent cutlers, for example, made knives for their factors that were stamped with his name. Later, as the disadvantages of such outworking of labor became clear, many factors converted their warehouses into large workshops where all operations would be carried out simultaneously in the same place — the factory.

The world's first pocketknife manufacturing factories were set-up in France during the eighteenth century. These used water-powered machinery to make mass-produced, inexpensive, folding penny knives with no backsprings. Solingen followed, creating the first modern pocket cutlery factory in 1805, but still using the outworking system of independent cutlers for a handcrafted effect, a system still in use to this day. Cutlery factories were also built in Sheffield, England between 1823 and 1826. An account of the methods used there, recorded in *The Practical Tourist* by Zachariah Allen, influenced the development of similar factories in the United States during the 1830s

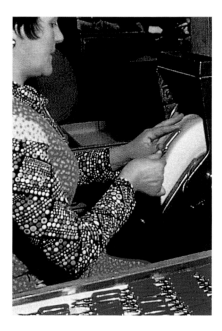

Above **One of the many stages in assembling the Victorinox "Swiss Army" knives.**

and 40s, and perhaps explains the peak amount of Sheffield cutlery sold in the United States in 1835.

The construction of large cutlery factories naturally led to rivalry over which was the biggest. Originally, the Sheaf Works factory in Sheffield was the biggest, but it was soon surpassed by others. Today, the world's largest cutlery factory is Imperial Schrade's 500,000 square foot facility in New York.

SEQUENCE BOARDS

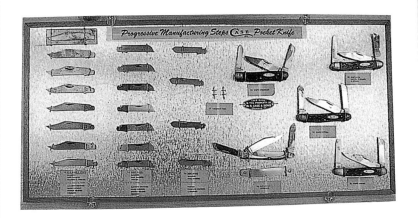

One of the oldest sales aids in cutlers' shops is the "sequence-of-manufacture" board. A sequence board is a series of identical knives, or the component parts thereof, each carried one step nearer to completion than the previous one. The first steps in a sequence board usually show the cutler's raw materials, while the last step is usually the finished cutlery item. In between, each piece or assembly fixed to the board demonstrates stages in the manufacturing process. These boards were used to sell individual knives and entire collections to consumers and retailers. Many manufacturers displayed sequence boards in their factory showrooms, sales offices, exhibition showcases, trade shows, and world fairs. Original sequence boards are one of the most sought-after items by knife collectors.

The sequence board shown above courtesy of its present owner, Smoky Mountain Knife Works, in Sevierville, Tennessee, which has hundreds of antique cutlery-advertising items on public display.

Multiblades and Gadget Knives

For as long as cutlers have been making folding knives, they have been working out ways to include other tools to fit with the blades in the handles. The most obvious non-blade tool that was included in pocketknives was the leather punch, a sharp tool essential for mending broken harnesses.

By the eighteenth century, cutlers were including an array of specialized blades and tools in folding knives. The ultimate was Joseph Rodgers & Sons Year Knife. Begun in 1822, it had 1,822 different blades with one more added every year until 1970!

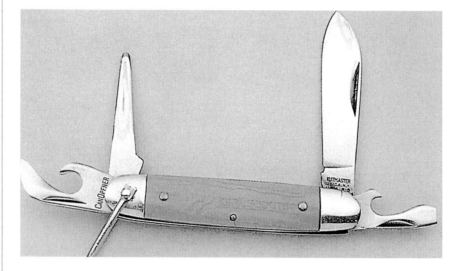

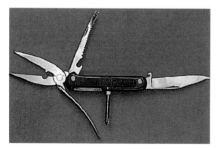

Above Kutmaster, 3 ³/₈ in (8.6cm), green-plastic handles with hot-stamp shield, four blades.

Left German Pirate logo combination knife, green horn handles. Blades: spear master blade, small screw driver/cap-lifter, lobster manicure blade, magnifier.

FOLDING KNIVES

Blades and tools used in folding knives

Leather punch ▪ Harness mending bolts ▪ Belt punch ▪ Gimlet ▪ Awl ▪ Typesetter's punch ▪ Quill pen blade ▪ Pen machine ▪ Letter opener ▪ Marlinespike ▪ Rope blade ▪ Weaver's hook ▪ Seam ripper ▪ Button hook ▪ Manicure blade ▪ Corn blade ▪ Scissors ▪ Spatula ▪ Metal saw ▪ Cockspur saw ▪ Spey blade ▪ Castrating hook ▪ Seton needle ▪ Scalpel ▪ Fleam ▪ Hoof-pick ▪ Dog-stripping comb ▪ Horticultural budding and grafting blade ▪ Grafting spud ▪ Cotton sampling blade ▪ Maize blade ▪ Pruning hook ▪ Pruning shears ▪ Weed digger ▪ Cigar cutter ▪ Cigar punch ▪ Cigar stub fork ▪ Cigar box opener ▪ Cigar box hammer ▪ Pipe tamper ▪ Pipe bowl reamer ▪ Snuff box ▪ Game counter ▪ Dice cup ▪ Fruit blade ▪ Nut and seed pick ▪ Fork ▪ Spoon ▪ Ear spoon ▪ Corkscrew ▪ Wire cutter ▪ Whistle

Pull-out implements in handles

▪ Toothpick ▪ Tweezers ▪ Lancet ▪ Dividers ▪ Cigar punch mechnism ▪ Fly-tying vise ▪ Sharpening steel

Tool kit Interchangeable blades

▪ Cutting blades ▪ Files ▪ Saws ▪ Screwdrivers ▪ Gimlet ▪ Punch ▪ Chisel ▪ Ruler ▪ Tin- and bottle- openers ▪ Cork pullers ▪ Hammer ▪

Tools for gadget-type folding-knives

▪ Alligator wrench ▪ Awl ▪ Belt punch ▪ Bird gutting-hook ▪ Bottle-cap lifter ▪ Button cutter ▪ Can opener ▪ Carriage key

▪ Castrating hook ▪ Champagne wire-cutter ▪ Cigar box hammer ▪ Cigar box opener ▪ Cigar cutter ▪ Cigar punch ▪ Cigar stub fork ▪ Cockspur saw ▪ Cork-pulling hook ▪ Corkscrew ▪ Corn blade ▪ Cotton-sampling blade ▪ Crescent wrench ▪ Dagger blade ▪ Dice cup ▪ Dog-stripping comb ▪ Drawing compass ▪ Dynamite-cap crimper ▪ Ear spoon ▪ Electrical-wire stripper ▪ Feeler gauges ▪ Fish gaff ▪ Fish scaler ▪ Fleam ▪ Fly-tying vise ▪ Fork ▪ Fuse cutter ▪ Game counter ▪ Gimlet ▪ Grafting spud ▪ Gutting blade ▪ Harness-mending bolts ▪ Hatchet ▪ Hoof pick ▪ Hook disgorger ▪ Hook hone ▪ Horticultural budding and grafting blade ▪ Ink-eraser blade ▪ Key-ring ▪ Leather punch ▪ Letter opener ▪ Magnetic compass ▪ Magnifying glass ▪ Maize blade ▪ Manicure blade and file ▪ Marlinespike ▪ Metal saw ▪ Oyster opener ▪ Pencil sharpener ▪ Pen ▪ Pen machine ▪ Pipe-bowl reamer ▪ Pipe tamper ▪ Pinfire-blank pistol ▪ Pistol ▪ Pliers ▪ "Pres-to-lite" key ▪ Pruning hook ▪ Pruning shears ▪ Quill-pen blade ▪ Race ▪ Rope blade ▪ Ruler ▪ Saw for bone and wood ▪ Scalpel ▪ Scissors ▪ Screwdriver ▪ Seam ripper ▪ Secton needle ▪ Shotgun-choke tube wrench ▪ Shotgun-shell extractors ▪ Fruit blade ▪ nut and seed pick ▪ Siren ▪ Skeleton key ▪ Skinning blade ▪ Snuff box ▪ Spatula or palette knife ▪ Spey blade ▪ Spoon ▪ Spring balance ▪ Stanhope lens with miniature photos ▪ Tape measure ▪ Typesetter's punch ▪ Weaver's hook ▪ Weed digger ▪ Whistle ▪ Wire cutter

Types of Pocketknives

Despite disagreement between experts, all pocketknives can be divided into three basic types on the basis of their structure. These three types are jackknives, penknives, and multiblades.

Jackknives and Penknives

Jackknives are stout and simply made. As a rule, a jackknife has its two to three blades in one end of the handle. Penknives are delicate and finely made. They generally have two to four blades in both ends. Some penknives include a nail-file manicure blade.

Just to make life interesting, there are exceptions to both of these rules. Stout knives with a large blade in each end are called double-end jackknives. Very small knives with a single, tiny blade in one end are the original penknives, designed for sharpening quill pens. To avoid

Below **The Penknife category includes the subcategory of whittler. Below are the Remington swell-center whittler, pearl handle and Wharncliffe whittler, bone handle.**

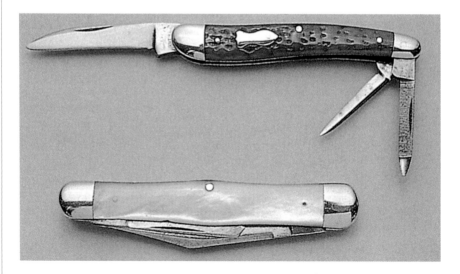

JACKKNIVES

Notes: (FH = large version used as folding hunter die) (DE = also used as a double-end jackknife die)
- Equal-End Jack (DE) Sunfish (Elephant Toenail) (DE only) ▪ Slim Equal-End Jack
- Regular Jack Electrician's Knife, Barlow Knife, Boy's Knife, No. 2 Scout Knife, English Jack (FH), Stabber pattern ▪ Slim Jack (Slim Regular Jack) Melon Tester, Physician's Knife ▪ Curved Regular Jack (FH) Rope Knife ▪ Sleeveboard Jack US WWI Electrician's Knife ▪ Jumbo Jack (large Sleeveboard) (DE) ▪ Curved Jack (the traditional English farmer's knife) Pruning Knife, Maize (grain sorghum) Knife, Cotton Sampler, Rope Knife, Whaler ▪ Swayback Jack ▪ Congress Jack
- Crown Jack (also called "Coffin Jack")
- Swell-End Jack ("Tear Drop")
- Swell-Center Jack ("Coke Bottle") (FH)
- Balloon Jack (DE) Platt's Sunfish (DE only) ▪ Swell-Center Regular Jack (FH) Trapper, Large Trapper ▪ Gunstock Jack Gunstock Budding Knife ▪ Premium Jack (DE) Premium Trapper (DE)
- Gunstock Premium Jack ▪ Serpentine Jack Peanut, Whamcliffe Jack (DE)
- Slim Serpentine Jack Light Trapper
- Eureka Jack (Swell-Center Serpentine Balloon Jack) (DE) ▪ Canoe (DE)
- Surveyor (Swell-Center Canoe) (DE) ▪ Fishtail Jack ▪ Fish Jack ▪ Tickler (Powder Horn) Fish Knife ▪ Clasp type (FH only)

PENKNIVES

Note: (WH = also used as whittler die)
- Senator Pen (Equal-End) (WH)
- Sleeveboard Pen (WH) Jumbo (WH only), Physician's (WH) ▪ Oval Pen (also called "Cigar," "Anglo-Saxon Knife") (WH) ▪ "Gunstock" Pen ▪ Congress Pattern (WH) Tobacco Knife ▪ Crown Pen (also known as "Coffin Pen") (WH) ▪ Modern Crown Pen ▪ Swell-Center Pen (including "Balloon Pen") (WH) Jenny Lind ▪ Premium Serpentine Pen ▪ Wharncliffe Pattern (WH) ▪ Dog-Leg Serpentine Pen (WH) ▪ Swell-Center Serpentine Pen (WH) Norfolk Pattern (WH only) ▪ Swell-Center Congress Knife (Sway-Back Pen) (WH)

Above Victorinox "Classic," equal-end lobster penknife.

Above A Ka-Bar limited-edition, lockback English jack with folding guard, stag-bone handles, and dog-head shield, lies above the James Ward & Co., rare American-made folding dirk with folding guard, horn handles, c1860s.

Above Case tested double-end premium jack, with rough-black composition handles.

Above Camillus easy-open regular jack with jigged-bone handles and steel mounts, made for the United States Army.

Above Miller Bros Cutlery, Meriden, CI, swell-center hunting knife, ebony. The use of tiny screws to retain the handles was a registered trademark of Miller Bros.

confusion, collectors now call these quill knives. In addition to ordinary penknives and quill knives, the penknife designation also embraces two distinctive sub-types. These are called whittlers (a modern collector name) and lobsters (a traditional cutlery-industry name).

Whittlers: A basic whittler is a three-blade knife. It has two backsprings that are separated at one end, but adjoin each other at the opposite end. A stout, master blade is mounted at the end, where the two springs touch. This blade is as thick as both the springs put together. Two shorter and thinner blades, one on each of the springs, are mounted at the other

end. This particular combination of blades makes larger whittlers well suited for whittling. However, the same construction was also used on smaller and more delicate three-blade penknives, which are also called whittlers by collectors.

While most pocketknife manufacture has been substantially automated, whittler construction still requires skilled handwork, and the pattern is now virtually extinct, except by a few handmakers or inexpensive German-made limited editions.

The earliest whittler-type knives, made in eighteenth century Paris, had a single spring split down the middle of most of the length, but using two

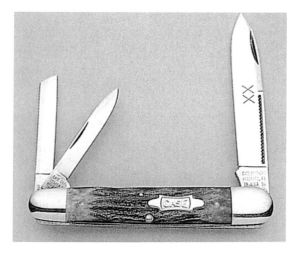

Left Case Brothers (Case Classic) 1990 limited-edition sleeveboard whittler, genuine stag (contract-made by Queen).

springs proved both easier and stronger. In some whittlers, a tapered center liner divides the two springs for most of their length. In others, a stubby catch divides only the two small blades from each other. A knife with three blades and three springs is definitely not considered to be a whittler, although Sheffield cutlers made five-blade whittlers, which are rare and very valuable.

Lobsters: A "lobster" is a penknife with blades both at the top and the bottom. Its springs are concealed inside the center of the handle. Before World War II, lobsters were among the most costly of pocketknives, but today, most collectors prefer larger knives that make for a more impressive display.

Folding Hunters: Modern-day knife collectors favor big folding knives, especially hunting knives. Folding hunters are generally 4–5in (10–12cm) long when closed. They have one or two large blades, and are a type of jackknife.

Classic folding hunters were made on a variety of standard handle dies: the swell-center or "Coke bottle," the swell-center regular, or "Trapper style," and four or five variations on the curved clasp knife. Many firms still make clasp-type folding hunters, but their popularity declined substantially after the 1960s.

Virtually all modern-style folding hunters, with their curved grip and stout metal frame, were either copied or derived from a single innovative prototype – the original Buck Model 110 folding hunter, which was introduced in 1962. Buck now makes many variations on its original design, and the 110 itself has seen quite an evolution of form and technology. Today, almost all factories design their knives, at least in part, on Buck's revolutionary 1962 design.

LOBSTER PENKNIFE

Note: (LWH = also made as lobster whittlers)

Oval Lobster (Charm Knife) ▪ Equal-End Lobster ▪ Sunfish Lobster ▪ Dolphin (Fish Candle-End Lobster) ▪ Sleeveboard Lobster (LWH) ▪ Sheffield Pattern Lobster ▪ Serpentine Lobster ▪ Serpentine Candle-End Lobster ▪ Gunstock Lobster Orange Blossom (LWH) ▪

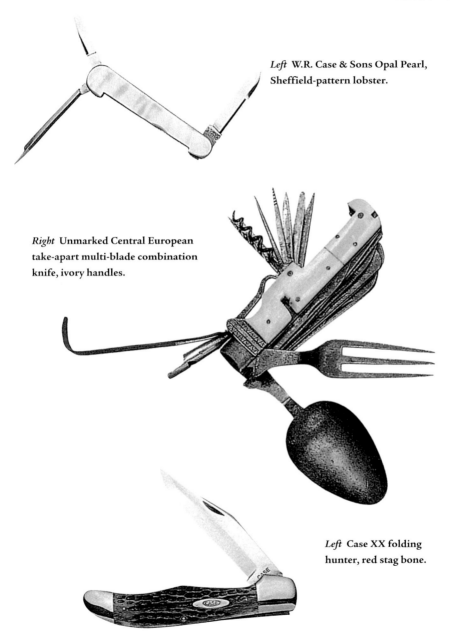

Left W.R. Case & Sons Opal Pearl, Sheffield-pattern lobster.

Right Unmarked Central European take-apart multi-blade combination knife, ivory handles.

Left Case XX folding hunter, red stag bone.

Multiblades

The category of multiblades includes all knives with three or more blades, of which one or more are gadget-type, such as can or bottle openers, leather punchers, corkscrews, forks, and spoons. Multiblades also include stout knives with three or more cutting blades, and a special-purpose blade, generally called the cattle knife. Other multiblade shapes are either very unusual, or are grouped into scout-utility knives, horseman's knives, sportsman's knives, stock knives, plier-and-wrench knives (including miner's dynamite knives), and fork-knife-spoon combinations.

Scout-Utility and Soldier's Knives

Perhaps the most familiar American multiblade is the scout-utility knife. This has four blades, in the same equal-end handle as the standard cattle knife, from which it was derived. There are over 30 different official Boy Scout knives, more than a dozen official Girl Scout knives, and at least five official Campfire Girls' knives in this pattern. Millions of American Scouts and ordinary consumers have used these knives since their introduction in 1910; American soldiers and marines have also used them since the United States Army adopted the pattern in 1941. British and Commonwealth scout and military folding knives,

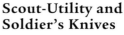

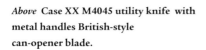

Above Case XX M4045 utility knife with metal handles British-style can-opener blade.

Right Imperial five-blade, official Boy Scout knife, Delrin plastic handles.

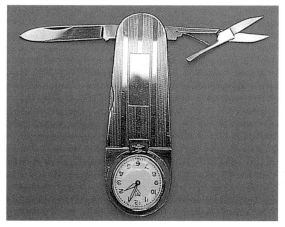

Above Unmarked Central European horseman's knife with genuine stag handles. Blades: clip master blade, pen blade, combination saw, can-opener, scissors, hoof-pick with attached carriage key, hollow leather punch, and corkscrew.

Left Latima, Italy pocket-watch and knife, stainless steel handles.

on the other hand, derived from eighteenth century sailors' jackknives, but now have many similar features to their American counterparts.

American sailors used British-style sailors' jackknives until World War I, when a smaller, American version was adopted. In World War II, the United States Navy switched to fixed-bladed knives, except for medical staff, who used utility knives, and lifeboat stores, which employed folding rope knives. Allied special operations units

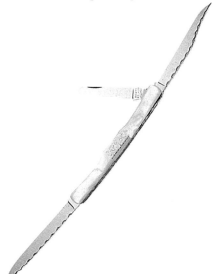

Above Digby's, Kelham Island (Sheffield), contemporary deluxe presentation knife, with engraving and filework. Note pearl used for the handle.

during World War II commissioned a wide variety of knives for secret missions, from both American and British cutlery firms. Most were unmarked and had fixed blades, but some, including a distinctive, all-metal, pliers-type multiblade, similar to a miner's dynamite knife that incorporated a can-opener and three hacksaw blades, were folding knives.

Sportsman's Knives: Sportsman's knives are elaborate multiblades with a multitude of specialized blades. Amongst the most familiar sportsman's knives are the Swiss Army knives, made both by Elsener/Victorinox of Ibach and by Wenger of Delemont, and imitated by scores of firms worldwide.

Today, Swiss Army knives are made in dozens of different models, but in the past, the range saw greater variety of type in terms of size, shape, blade type, and sheer complexity. Some late eighteenth and early nineteenth century horseman's knives (the name for sportsman's knives with a folding hoof-pick on the back) even had blades folding up inside other blades.

In recent times, red plastic is used for the handle on these knives. In the old days, genuine stag was standard, but metal, bone, horn, ivory, tortoise-shell, and pearl were options as well.

Above German-style folding Bowie, "Le Louis d'Or" (gold-coin brand) made in France, stag handles.

Handle Dies and Named Patterns

The sheet-metal frame pieces of a pocketknife handle, which are known as liners, were stamped with a set of steel dies, and each different shape came to be called a handle die. Every jackknife and penknife handle die has a name. The ones we are familiar with today are the result of the standardization of patterns that developed between 1840 and 1890. The handle dies before that period probably had names too, but most of them seem to have been lost.

The term "handle die" essentially refers to the shape of a pocketknife's handle. "Pattern" is even more specific, indicating a particular combination of handle die and blades. In a cutlery catalog, a particular pattern number specifies the handle die, size, blades, mount materials, and handle material.

British Pocketknife Patterns: While much of Sheffield's output went to American and Commonwealth markets, the city's singlemost important cutlery market was Britain itself, especially after 1891. Every pocketknife firm in Sheffield selected "town patterns," or pocketknife patterns typical of Sheffield.

The best-known town pattern was the horseman's multiblade. At its most basic, this pattern includes a spear blade, pen blade, and saw on top, with a corkscrew, augur, punch, and combined hoof-pick-nutcracker on the bottom. Other town patterns

Above Hoffritz (United States retailer) German-made folding pruning knife with pruning blade, pruning shears, and pruning saw, with wood handles.

included the senator and congress penknives (originally developed for the American trade), the sailor's knife used by the military, the "church window," and the curved jackknife with sheep foot blade, favored by farmers in the Channel Islands, Orkneys, Dover, and Donegal.

The English version of the folding hunting knife was a simple, regular or sleeveboard pattern, 4–7in (10–17.5cm) long when closed, with a single locking clip or spear-point blade. The favorite lobster pattern in Britain, known as the Sheffield-pattern lobster in the United States, was a bolstered sleeveboard with an extra-wide manicure blade set into the back. As late as 1970, Wostenholm's made large quantities of Sheffield-pattern lobsters to be sold by the infamous jeweler, Cartier.

French Pocketknife Patterns: France boasts of an ancient cutlery industry and a wide array of traditional pocketknife patterns. Best known are the Opinels from Cognin. Standard Opinels, sold worldwide, are wood-handled penny knives with a rotating-ferrule lock. Deluxe horn- and ivory-handled models made for collectors are sold by Courty et Fils in Paris.

Almost as familiar is the Laguiole, a locking-clasp knife with a slender, yatagan-style blade, which often has a corkscrew in the back. Pierre Calmels makes the genuine article in the town of Laguiole, where his grandfather created the pattern, but the best-known exported Laguioles come from G. David.

The French pradel, named after a nineteenth century family of Thiers cutlers, is strikingly similar to the most basic American jackknife, the Barlow, named after a seventeenth century family of Sheffield, England cutlers. Pradel is the name for a barehead, regular jack with a single, short-pull spear blade. The

Left **H. G. Long & Co., Sheffield, sportsman's combination knife with genuine stag handles. Blades: patent, adjustable, shotshell extractor, spear-master blade, large buttoner for gaiters, and corkscrew.**

Mediterranean island of Corsica, which is French territory, boasts its own distinctive style of "Vendetta Corse" folding knives. These self-guard clasp knives with long bolsters have deadly, needle-sharp blades. They are made in a wide range of sizes, both in Thiers and on Corsica.

German Pocketknife Patterns: For an entire millennium, German cutlers were the swordsmiths of the world, and for more than a century, they were the pocket cutlers of the world as well. From their workshops in Solingen came endless varieties of pocketknives. Most of these were made for export, with the more limited variety created for domestic sale.

The most typical German pocketknives are the large, stag-handled, folding hunters. These were made in many sizes and shapes, and with auxiliary blades — usually a saw and a corkscrew. Also typical was the clasp knife with a horn, stag, or deer-foot handle (the latter complete with fur and hoof), which was the ancestor of the American pattern called the "tickler" or "toothpick." An inexpensive, all-metal version of this knife, made by Kauffmann, has been popular in Germany since World War I.

Traditional Japanese Pocketknife: Today, most of the pocketknives made in Japan are copied from American or European prototypes, but Japan does have its own traditional style of folding knife. This all-metal Higonokami knife boasts a laminated-steel blade with a cut-off point and super-sharp cutting edge. The blade is saber ground on the front and flat on the back. High-quality examples are signed with a calligraphic flourish, both on the flat of the blade and on the steel handle.

Fancy-Handled Pocketknives

In most pocketknives, the important part is the blade. The blades are the business end, the parts that do the work. There is a class of pocketknife, however, whose principal work is communication rather than cutting. Thus the shape, artwork, and inscriptions on the handles of some pocketknives are more important than the blades, and often it is the handles that do the real work.

Figural Knives: Figural knives are the oldest type of pocketknives. Most ancient-Roman pocketknives are figural knives whose handles are miniature sculptures of people, the human body, animals, or objects.

Above Stainless steel (Japan), equal-end lobster penknife with stainless-steel handles. High-quality steel handles are often signed with a calligraphic flourish.

Advertising Knives: Advertising knives are usually given by business firms as mementos or presents, to remind clients and potential customers about the firm. This usually acts as a clever marketing device, with their name or trademark appearing on the handle.

Character and Celebrity Knives: Character and celebrity knives depict popular fictional or fantasy characters, or real-life popular heroes. However, the heyday of character pocketknives was from the late 1930s until the early 1960s, and few are produced today.

The names and faces of political figures appeared on American pocketknives early in the nineteenth century, and the use of pocketknives in political campaigns continues today.

Perhaps the first entertainment celebrity to endorse the use of his likeness on a pocketknife was William F. "Buffalo Bill" Cody, whose Wild-West show delighted big-city audiences on both sides of the Atlantic.

Photographs of sports heroes have also adorned pocketknife handles since 1910. The first sports star to make an actual endorsement deal for a pocketknife was the legendary baseball player Babe Ruth, in 1930. He received a royalty for allowing his autograph to be reproduced on a baseball-bat figural knife.

Commemorative Knives: Commemorative knives, inspired by commemorative stamps and coins, record important anniversaries.

Souvenir Knives: Souvenir knives, bought as souvenirs from the location where they were made, are an old tradition. American visitors to Sheffield bought knives as mementos in the 1830s, while visitors to San Francisco in the 1870s bought knives made there by Michael Price or Will & Finck. However, knives made and explicitly marked as souvenirs date back little more than a century. Generally, they are inexpensive, and are designed to appeal to the mass market.

Limited-Edition Knives: Limited-edition knives are those made expressly as collector items. Sometimes they are replicas of antique knives, and some are unofficial commemoratives. Their quality ranges from shoddy to very fine,

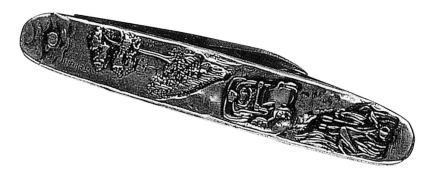

Above **Empire Knife Co., West Winsted, CT, silver-handled figural knife.**

Left New York Knife Co., Walden, NY, dog figural knife, with carved-pearl handles.

Right Unmarked airplane figural knife.

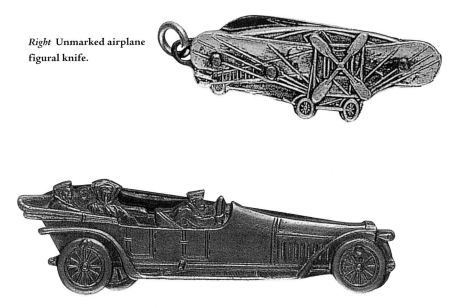

Above Germania Cutlery Works car-design figural knife, imported by Adolph Kastor & Bros., New York.

with the latter always a better bargain than the former, regardless of price!

Of special interest are limited-edition knife club knives, commissioned by local or regional collector clubs and offered for sale to their members.

Types of Construction

The production technology of fancy-handled knives has evolved over the years. These knives were usually intended for mass-market sales, or to be given away, so low cost was usually a prime consideration. Technological innovations were often applied to advertising and souvenir-knife

construction before they were applied to ordinary pocketknives.

The following list is a roughly chronological account of the types of handle construction used on fancy knives, along with comments on their application and significance.

Right **Ka-Bar limited edition congress knife, red stag-bone handles.**

Above Schrade commemorative knives including (clockwise from top left): Schrade Cutlery's 85th anniversary, 1989; Federal duck-stamp, 1990/1991, United States. National Park Service 75th anniversary, 1991; 50th anniversary of United States entry into World War II, 1991.

Pressed-Horn Handles: Low-relief scenes were pressed into horn handles using steel dies and steam pressure. These were probably the first mass-produced illustrated handles, and were substantially cheaper to make than earlier figural knives, which were individually handcarved.

Engraved Ivory, Pearl, or Bone Handles: Most of this work, which was still being crafted in the 1930s, was done by hand, and is only found on high-quality advertising knives generally given to executives.

Cast- or Coined-Metal Handles: This technology was rapidly developed during the first year or two of the Civil War (1860–1865). The typical, cheap soldier's jackknife of that period had stamped-brass or cast-iron handles, advertising the firm that made the knife. In the 1870s and 1880s, James D. Frary of Bridgeport, Connecticut, made

a large business of cheap, pictorial pocketknives with cast-pewter handles. In 1886, after aluminum had become available commercially, P. Daniel Peres specialized in commemorative, souvenir, advertising, and political pocketknives with highly detailed, aluminum handles stamped in deep relief. Thereafter, many firms in Germany, France, and the United States offered an endless variety of embossed handles in a wide range of metals. Most knives with unplated brass handles are, in fact, modern replicas or counterfeits.

Molded-Celluloid or Composition Handles: The invention of celluloid and other plastics in the late nineteenth century allowed a

renaissance of figural knives. With moldable plastics for handles, these could be easily mass produced instead of handcarved.

Clear-Celluloid Picture Handles:
Reuben and Henry Landis of Canton, Ohio, patented a method of bonding photographs or other pictures to clear celluloid to make durable, picture-handled pocketknives. From this grew an important segment of the American pocket-cutlery industry of the Golden Age — the novelty and custom illustration knives, produced by firms such as Novelty Cutlery Co., Canton Cutlery Co., Aerial Cutlery Co., and Golden Rule Cutlery Co. These custom pocketknives sold by

the millions, from the 1880s up until the 1930s.

Enameled-Metal Handles: Cloisonné-like enamel-handled pocketknives were developed in Solingen around 1890. Their ornate, gilt-brass frames were filled with multicolored enamels, creating a gorgeous effect. Often, these knives, as well as some with engraved-pearl or ivory handles, incorporated tiny Stanhope lens "peepholes," containing miniature

photographs. These knives were very expensive, and their principal consumer was the American brewer, Adolphus Busch, who liked to give them away to people he met on his extensive world travels.

Color-Etched Metal Handles: Techniques that combined etching with enameling and selective electroplating were developed in Sweden and Germany early in the twentieth century. They were used to

Below **Annual "Schrade Scrimsaw" wildlife limited-edition set.**

produce a wide variety of pocketknife handles with colorful, attractive, inexpensive, and relatively durable pictures, designs, and advertising messages. These knives are not yet appreciated by collectors as much as they deserve to be.

Stamped or Lithographed Celluloid and Plastic Handles: These very simple techniques for decorating handles have been around for over a century, and are today the most widely used. They can vary from a spartan, single

line of type to elaborate full-color and full-coverage illustrations.

Metal Inlaid Celluloid or Plastic Handles: The technique of molding silhouettes or words, cut from thin sheets of nickel silver, into white or imitation-pearl celluloid pocketknife handles was developed in Germany, sometime around 1930. Today, this technique is used on Swiss pocketknives with solid-color plastic handles.

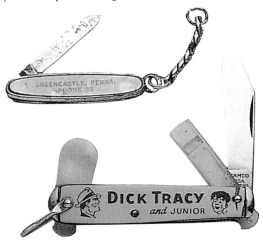

Top Ambassador (Colonial Knife Co., Providence, RI) miniature key ring knife advertising Greencastle Livestock Market, Greencastle, Pa. "cracked ice" (imitation pearl) celluloid handles.

Bottom Camco (Camillus) "Dick Tracy and Junior" character knife with magnifying glass and whistle.

Handcrafted Folding Knives

If you have only ever seen pocketknives for sale in hardware, cutlery, or sports shops, you are likely to be shocked the first time you see handmade pocketknives on sale at a knife show, art gallery, or jewelry shop. As a rule of thumb, the price of a reasonable, handmade folding knife by a less prominent knife maker is ten times the price of a factory pocketknife of similar size. A comparable folding knife by a world-renowned maker might cost ten times more. To understand this phenomenon, it helps to have a historical perspective on handmade folding knives.

The Golden Age: The half-century between 1890 and the 1940s was regarded the Golden Age of the American pocketknife. Beginning in the 1890s, protective tariffs curtailed the access of foreign cutlery firms to the American market. The American firms that had lobbied for higher duties then moved in aggressively to fill the gap. Not only did they take over the United States market from their English and German rivals, but they also recruited some of the most talented Sheffield and Solingen pocket cutlers.

Thus reborn, the American pocketknife industry was a conjoining of the best of Old-World handcraftsmanship with the best of American industrial organization, marketing, and innovation. The result for the American pocketknife buyer was a rich bounty of wonderful folding knives. This development was interrupted briefly by World War I, but was back on track by 1920.

Before 1940, the best folding knives were, in fact, handmade. Back then, only a few makers made small numbers of indestructible folding knives by hand.

Right **Made in United States, a Tickler under clear celluloid handle.**

Above **"The Primate Knife."** Folding knife by Ron Lake, 3 ¹/₂ in (8.15cm) long closed, with gold-engraved eyeglass screwdriver in the handle. Inlaid with gold and engraved by Ron Smith.

The Dark Age: After World War II, however, the story was quite different. Many of the important pre-war pocketknife manufacturers had left the business, and most remaining pocket cutlery firms had experienced four years of the low standards, limited varieties, and guaranteed profits of war contracts. During the war, however, while what remained of the cutlery industry was cranking out millions of adequate knives, hundreds of individual knife makers found the opportunity to handcraft thousands of better-than-ordinary knives (most of which were fixed blade knives). After the war, the demand for handmade knives, eventually declined.

The Renaissance: In the early 1970s, a few new craftsmen — including Ron Lake, Bob Hayes, Jess Horn, Jimmy

Lile, Paul Poehlmann, Barry Wood, and Robert Ogg — made a solid start that earned them a growing customer following.

Two decades ago, handmade knives were virtually synonymous with fixed-blade knives. There is still some interest today in handmade fixed blades of the very best quality, but most collectors are interested strictly in handmade folding knives.

Looking at Folding Knives: Very few of the top folding-knife makers do real custom work to customer designs. Some customers have their knives customized with fine engravings, but even the most amazing engravings do not enhance resale value on the knife-collector market. In the knife — as in the jewelry market, however, superb engravings are almost obligatory.

Some handcrafted-knife makers sell directly to customers, but it is much better to buy through dealers who specialize in handmade knives.

Fashions in Folding Knives: Knife collecting is governed by fashions and fads. This is especially true for the collection of contemporary, handmade knives, because knife makers can, and do, invent new fashions.

Some years ago, the hottest trend in folding knives was the innovation of blade locking mechanisms. While interest in novel locks still remains, the most recent trend is simplicity of line and flawless execution.

Exotic metals — gold, platinum, and iridium — enjoy a current vogue. Titanium, niobium, and even aluminum can be toned to bright colors with heat, electricity, and chemicals. Michael and Patricia Walker pioneered this technique on folding knives, along with a much-improved version of the 1906

Cattaraugus "Liner Lock," and attracted many imitators.

One trend that is on the rise is that of the small, yet exquisite and expensive, handmade Gentlemen's knife. Most successful so far have been small jackknives with extra touches, such as gold fittings. A few makers have tried penknife and multiblade designs, but many buyers are not ready to spend large sums on little knives, and most makers have not reached the Golden-Age level of quality in small knives.

Below **"Gentleman's Folding Knife" by Ron Lake. Total length when open 4 ½ in (11cm). 18-carat gold frame and bail, pearl-handle inlays.**

Popular Pocketknife Brands

A pocketknife's story can be read on its blade's tangs — the unsharpened extension fixed into the knife's handle.

Blade tangs are usually stamped with the name or trademark of the firm that distributed the knife. This is important because though a knife may have value in itself, most collectors care about the brand names stamped on its tangs, since some brands make better quality knives. Brands also matter to those who like to collect things in complete sets, as a knife's brand can tell them if it belongs with their other knives. Moreover, the knife's brand indicates its approximate age, and where and how it was sold as well as who owned it originally.

The following section introduces you to some of the most popular brands of knives, and also various styles of knives produced. These include some of the most famous brands in the United States and Europe, as well as some of the more specialty-type knives.

Famous American Brands

Case Brothers/W R. Case & Sons: The original Case Bros. firm was formed in 1896, when three Case brothers began a wholesale cutlery firm in Little Valley, New York. Although

their designs were at first contracted out, by 1900, they were manufacturing their own knives, straight razors, and hones. This lasted until 1915, but in 1902, their nephew, Russell Case, opened his own firm, naming it W R. Case & Sons Cutlery Co. He later opened a

Top Case XX USA 6-dot (1974) premium jack, red jigged-bone handles.

Above Large Case store display knife, 11¼ in (28cm) long, closed, slick, black composition handles.

W.R. CASE & SONS

The Case brand has been phenomenally popular in the United States for over 25 years. One reason for this is in the 1960s, when collecting pocketknives first became popular, Case offered a diverse, high-quality line of traditional designs with deluxe, natural handles of pearl and stag. Because Case changed its blade-tang stampings regularly over the years, it has been easy for collectors to date them. In addition, Case knives were widely available.

Case/Bradford, PA This was used as a two-line tang stamping from 1905–1920. Some recent reissue collector knives also bear this stamping, but their materials and finish identify them as modern.

Case/Tested XX Tested by collectors, this mark (or slight variations of it) was standard from around 1920–1940. This brand is widely counterfeited, so beware.

Case/XX Called Double X by collectors, this two-line mark was standard on Case pocket knives from the postwar resumption of commercial marketing during 1945–1965.

Case XX/row of dots with runic "SS" in center/USA Called Lightning S by collectors, the runic "SS" stands for "stainless steel," and the amount of dots specify the year in which the knife was made, starting from 1890 through to 1990 (10 dots = 1980; 9 dots = 1981).

*Other versions include *Case XX/Made in USA* (1965–1970; called Case USA by collectors) *Case XX/Made in USA/above a tiny row of dots* (1970–1980).

| 1905-1920 | 1920-1940/41 | 1945-1965 | 1980-1990 |

Left Western States Cutlery
Co., Boulder, CO, Dox Fish
Gaff angler's knife.

different factory with H. N. Platts
in Bradford, Pennsylvania —
the knives made there excite the
greatest interest.

Western States Cutlery Co.: This firm
originated in New York in 1896, when
an emigrant cutler from Sheffield,
Charles W. Platts, decided to start
his own pocketknife company. C. W.
Platts & Sons was taken over in 1900
by his second son, Harvey Nixon
Platts, who moved the company to
Colorado, and changed its name
to Western States Cutlery and
Manufacturing Co. In 1920, this
company initiated the manufacture
of pocketknives in the American

West, adding hunting knives to its
product range in 1928. It changed
names again between 1956 and 1990,
first to Western Cutlery Co. and then
to Coleman-Western, but its most
popular products predate 1941.

Union Cutlery Co.: Wallace
and Emerson Brown began
manufacturing and importing
pocketknives and razors under the
name Brown Bros. Mfg. Co. in
Pennsylvania in 1890. They later
changed the company's name to
Union Cutlery Co. The firm moved
to a new factory in New York, in
1912, where it enjoyed great success
through its association with the

Case Bros, producing pocketknives and hunting knives under the trademark KA-BAR.

KA-BAR/Kabar Cutlery Co.: The name KA-BAR is commonly associated with the United States Marine Corps 1219C2 (Navy Mark 2) combat knife, introduced in 1943. It was developed by Camillus, but bore the KA-BAR stamping; both Camillus and KA-BAR versions of this design are still sold commercially.

There are also some classic KA-BAR knives, whose front handles are inlaid with a shield in the shape of a dog's head. Union Cutlery's trademark KA-BAR name was changed to Kabar Cutlery Co. in 1951, which is a watershed date for collectors, since later stampings are considered less desirable. The older KA-BAR stamping is still used on limited reissues of classic knives, but the current Kabar-brand knives are either made under contract, or are imported. Kabar Cutlery became a division of Cole National Corp. in Cleveland, Ohio in 1966; its other brands include Khyber, Sabre, and Monarch.

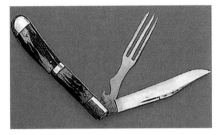

Above Union Cutlery Co., Olean, NY, Model 2291 K&F "slot knife" take-apart knife and fork, with genuine stag handles.

Below Ka-Bar Olean, NY gunstock jack, 1980 limited edition.

Cattaraugus Cutlery Co.: This Little Valley, New York-based firm began as J.B.E. Champlin & Son, a wholesale importer of German cutlery. In 1886, the founder changed the name to Cattaraugus (after the county's name), and began manufacturing cutlery as a supplement to their imports. This included pocketknives, razors, scissors, and, in 1925, hunting knives. The latter were produced as a joint venture between Case and Cattaraugus in the Kinfolks factory in Little Valley, which later became an independent company also producing pocketknives. Cattaraugus was famous for its WWII 2250 Commando knives,

aircrew-survival folding machetes, and TL-29 electrician's knives, with their innovative liner-lock. Cattaraugus also made the knives for Admiral Richard E. Byrd's Antarctic expeditions. Later, the company focused mainly on fixed-blade kitchen knives with black, plastic handles and chrome-plated blades; its products are now less popular among collectors than they were 10–15 years ago.

Robeson Cutlery Co.: Millard Robeson first sold imported knives from his home in Elmira, New York. In 1894, he began to manufacture his own knives, eventually building factories

Right **Cattaraugus Cutlery Co., Little Valley, NY crescent wrench-knife with stag-bone handles.**

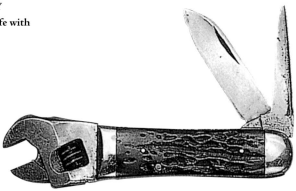

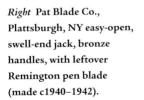

Below **Robeson No-Rustain lockback English jack with folding guard.**

in Rochester, Perry, and New York, to produce his Shuredge brand of pocketknives. When Emerson Case (the grandson of W.R.) became President of the company in 1940, he increased its prosperity by introducing stainless steel blades, now used in all pocketknife production. Robeson stopped manufacturing in 1960, but continued to sell contract-made Robeson knives until 1977. Robeson knives are not as valuable as Case of KA-BAR.

Remington U.M.C./Pal Blade Co.: Beginning in 1920, the Remington Arms-Union Metallic Cartridge Company produced pocketknives, along with WWI ammunition, in an ultramodern factory in Bridgeport, Connecticut. However, by 1925, its cutlery division had become the dominant maker of top-quality pocketknives in the United States. At its peak in 1931, the company was producing over 10,000 high-quality pocketknives a day, with over 1,000 different patterns (also hunting knives, household cutlery, and advertising and promotional

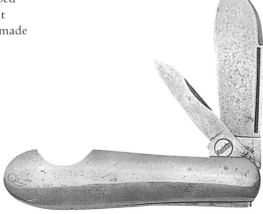

Right **Pat Blade Co., Plattsburgh, NY easy-open, swell-end jack, bronze handles, with leftover Remington pen blade (made c1940–1942).**

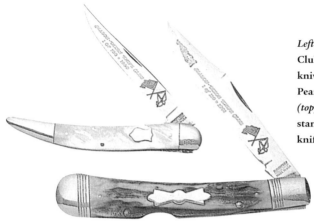

Left **Mason-Dixon Knife Club, 1990 and 1991 club knives by Winchester. Pearl-handled toothpick (*top*). Stag-handled, curved, standard hunting knife (*bottom*).**

materials that are as avidly collected as the knives themselves). In 1940, the company stopped cutlery production to resume work on defense materials, and its cutlery division was sold to Pal Blade Co. in Plattsburgh, New York. Yet, because of its previous glory and the famous name's link to gun collecting, Remington is one of the most sought-after brands today.

Remington Bullets: In 1922, Remington introduced the first of two dozen patterns of large, stout, sportsman's folding knives, each with a shield in the shape of a high-power rifle cartridge — hence, the collector's name of Remington Bullets. The initial "bullet" knife, the R1123 large trapper with jigged-bone handles, is the most popular. In 1982, replicas of the R1123 with plastic handles proved to be very successful, and

Remington have since issued a new replica bullet knife every year. These are now nearly as rare and valuable as the originals.

Winchester: Originally a firearms company based in Connecticut, Winchester went into the cutlery business after World War I, buying out existing firms and employing skilled staff from the Napanoch Knife Co., New York (a major, private-brand contractor founded in 1901). The Heming Brothers, who had invented the first successful automatic grinder in 1903, founded the Eagle Knife Co. in New Haven, which provided the technology for mass production. Original Winchester pocketknives are near the quality of Remington pocketknives, except for the cheap assortment knives made during the Depression. However, they are as

SECRET REVOLUTION

Both Remington and Winchester experimented with modernizing the manufacturing process after World War I. Remington tried to eliminate the extra steps and uncertain results of "chopping on" bolsters to handles, by substituting integral, drop-forged handle frames. Meanwhile, Winchester attempted to substitute forging in their first blades, with blanked-and-ground, chrome-vanadium tool steel for forged, high-carbon steel. However, neither firms' techniques were accepted by professional hardware buyers, who refused to tolerate new pocketknife technology, thus forcing both firms to revert to their original procedures. Despite this, both firms continued to develop new technology, but this time, they ensured that it did not show. Today, most pocketknife firms continue to hide most of their technological innovations under a veneer of traditional appearance.

Below **Remington 1993 Bullet knife.**

popular among collectors as Remington's are, and are also equally valuable.

E. C. Simmons — Keen Kutter and Oak Leaf: The best-known and most successful United States wholesale hardware firm was the E. C. Simmons Hardware Co. of St. Louis, Missouri, established in 1868. It was the first company to become incorporated, allowing employee profit sharing, and also the first to produce an illustrated catalog. Simmons bought key manufacturers to control the costs and supply of his two most popular brands of pocketknives, the Keen Kutter and Oak Leaf, making a huge profit by selling private brand merchandise to other firms. Simmons also acquired the Walden Knife Co. (Walden, New York) in 1902. Simmons merged with Winchester in 1922, but was later

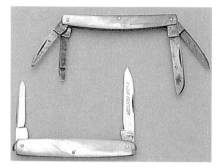

Above Two E. C. Simmons Keen Kutter pearl-handled penknives: a four-blade shadow congress *(top)*, and a senator with tip bolsters *(bottom)*.

absorbed by its long-term rival, Shapleigh Hardware Co.

New York Knife Co. — Hammer and Walkill River Works: Before the rise of Remington, New York Knife Co. in Walden, New York was the leading supplier of high-quality pocketknives to wholesale markets. The company supplied knives both under its popular Hammer brand, as well as other house-brand names. The company was the first to make the official Boy Scout knives, and also specialized in producing cheap, English-style knives with the Walkill River Works logo. The firm went out of business in 1930, and its Hammer logo was taken over by Imperial.

Queen Cutlery Co./Schaff & Morgan: This company's original founders, J. W. Schatt and C. B. Morgan, began as cutlery importers and jobbers in New York, where they opened a factory under their joint names. They later relocated to Titusville, Pennsylvania, where some of their supervisors set up the Queen City Cutlery Co. on the side, using Schatt & Morgan's components. By the time they were caught and fired, S & M was bankrupt, and Queen City took over its assets, changing its company name to Queen Cutlery Co. While Queen and Original S & M knives are popular with collectors, Queen is best known today as the contract manufacturer of some KA-BAR reissue Winchesters, and the Case Heritage series, also producing reissue S & M knives for collectors.

Ulster Knife Co.: In 1871, a group of Sheffield cutlers formed the Cooperative Knife Co. in Ulster County, New York. When this company failed, it was reorganized in 1876 under local banker Dwight Divine as the Ulster Knife Co., and soon became a leading, private-brand contractor of high-quality knives. It continued to use Sheffield-style handcrafted methods and quality up to 1941 despite the loss of profits, but was inevitably forced to sell.

Albert M. Baer bought the company and brought in specialists, who succeeded in transforming Ulster into the most modern cutlery plant in the world.

Kingston Cutlery Co.: After Pearl Harbor, the Army Advisory Board coordinated all United States cutlery firms to make millions of knives for the armed forces. In 1943, Albert Baer of Ulster Knife Co. and the owners of Imperial Knife Co. formed a joint venture called Kingston Knife Co., after an Ulster brand. Kingston produced utility knives throughout the war, later taking over Schrade Cutlery Co.

Schrade Cutlery Co.: George Schrade, founder of the Schrade Cutlery Co. in Walden, New York, was one of the most prolific inventors in American cutlery history. His Press-Button knife, introduced in 1892, was the

first switchblade suited to mass-production methods. Schrade also invented and manufactured automatic assembly machines for making pocketknife components, widely used across the United States and Europe. In addition to a full line of conventional knives, Schrade Cutlery Co. also made Safety Push-Button knives with a handle release, and a later model with a sliding safety latch near the button.

Imperial Knife Co.: Imperial Knife Co. was formed in 1916 in Providence, Rhode Island, by two Italian immigrants who had worked

Below Left **New York Knife Co., Walden, NY Model 135 rase knife with cocobolo handles.**

Below Right **Queen Cutlery Co., Titusville, PA sleeveboard jack Winterbottom-bone handles.**

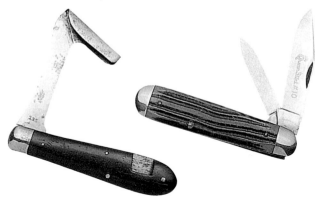

for the Empire Knife Co., in
Connecticut. During WWI, they made
vast numbers of little IKCO-brand
jackknives for the United States
Navy, but later specialized in skeleton
knives fitted with gold or silver
handles by jewelers, and low-cost,
mass-produced jackknives with
fancy handles, popular today with
cost-conscious collectors. In the
late 1930s, Imperial licensed the
technology for making cheap
pocketknives with hollow sheet-
steel handles covered with sheet
celluloid, from Solingen inventor
Ernst Lohr. This technology was
steadily improved in the next two
decades, and by the 1940s, Imperial
was producing 100,000 Jackmaster
Hammer Brand knives a day, replaced
by Diamond Edge knives in the
1960s. Their merger with Ulster Knife
Co. and Shrade in 1943 under the
title Imperial Knife Associated
Companies has made them the
world's leading cutlery manufacturer.

Camillus Cutlery Co.: In 1902, Adolph
Kastor, a leading New York City
cutlery importer and wholesaler,

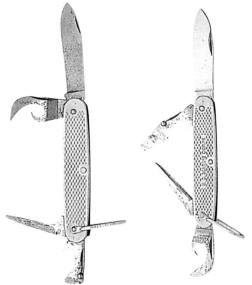

Above **Kingston (joint venture of Ulster and
Imperial) utility knife made for the United
States Marine Corps, World War II, and
Kingston utility knife made for the United
States Army, World War II.**

Below **Schrade Cutlery Co., Walden, NY
Safety "Push-Button" Knife, with
celluloid handles.**

bought a small pocketknife plant in Camillus, New York. Through diligent salesmanship of private-brand knives to emerging mass-market retail chains, Camillus soon became the leading American contract maker of private brands, a position it still holds. Camillus was also the leading maker of American character and figural pocketknives in the 1930s and 40s, and has been a leading supplier of deluxe advertising knives for companies such as Anheuser Busch and Coca-Cola; today, it makes the most popular limited-edition knives, including reissue Remingtons and wildlife or other collector specials.

Utica Culler Co. — Kutmaster and Jack Knife Ben: Though not as well known as some of its rivals, the Utica Cutlery Co. from upstate New York has been an important pocket cutlery firm since 1910. Its many well-known trademark brands include Agate Wood, American Maid, Feather-weight, Iroquois, Seneca, and Pocket Pard, but the best known brand by far was the Kutmaster, adopted in 1937. The company has long been an active private-brand contractor with

Chicago-based retailers, and is known for its production of Wards pocketknives for Montgomery Wards, and its famous Jack Knife Ben knives, which are in great demand by collectors. The company now specializes in pocketknives with

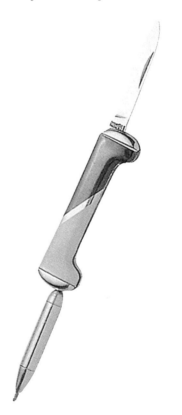

Right Imperial lobster penknife with Jackmaster sheet celluloid over hollow-steel shell handles, folding ballpoint pen.

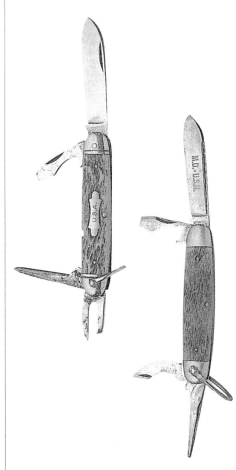

coined-metal handles, both under its own name and under contract.

Gerber Legendary Blades: In 1939, Joseph R. Gerber, an advertising man in Portland, Oregon, designed his first carving knife, which led him to open a factory producing carving and steak knives with cast-aluminum handles. Since the 1960s, Gerber began to make hunting knives and combat-survival knives. Gerber also imports smaller, folding knives which are from Japan, marketed under the names Silver Knight, as well as Gerber-Paul button-lock, folding knives, much in demand among United States collectors. The company is now owned by the Fiskars cutlery firm in Helsinki, Finland.

J. Russell & Co. — Russell Barlows: One of the first-recorded cutlery factories in the United States, the Greenfield River Works in Massachusetts, was built in 1834 by John Russell — maker of the famous Russell & Co. Barlow knives. These were so popular, especially in the South, that nearly every hardware and cutlery firm offered a selection. The firm made various knives until it merged with Harrington Cutlery in 1933; its last, authentic Russell Barlow was made in 1941. The knife's popularity lives on.

Above Left **Camillus Cutlery Co., Camillus, NY utility knife made for the United States Army, World War I.**

Above Right **Utica Cutlery Co., Utica, NY Kutmaster brand utility knife made for the Medical Department, United States Navy, World War II, used by Navy medics who served with the Marines.**

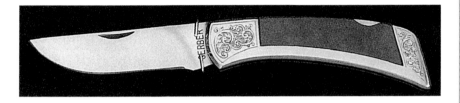

Above **Presentation-boxed, Gerber folding sportsman with engraved-brass frame and green jade-handle inlays.**

Buck knives: Another popular knife from the United States is the Buck Knife, a generic term deriving from the original Buck's Model 110 folding hunting knife with handmade, fixed blades. Their ancestor, Hoyt Heath Buck, had made the first Buck knives with fixed blades early in the century, and while they created their model as an improvement to his design, they were surprised at the knife's success and wide-ranging appeal. The Model 110, with its sturdy, lockback, folding mechanism, has now sold millions, and is the most successful new knife design of all time, as well as the most copied.

Al Mar Knives and Kershaw Cutlery Co.: These two companies were both founded by former Gerber employees in the 1970s. The companies primarily import knives from Japan, sold under the name

Silver Knight. Their knives are sold around the world, and are known to attract a great deal of interest from many pocketknife collectors.

Hardware Wholesalers

Hardware wholesaler house brands are an up-and-coming specialty in pocketknife collecting, largely because of their historical value. The evolution of hardware distribution was a key chapter in the economic development of North America, with its heyday lasting from 1840 to 1940, a time when every American and Canadian city, from the established East-coast states to the developing, Western - frontier states, had at least two or three wholesale hardware firms. These supplied local hardware and general merchandise shops within a 100-mile radius with a wide array of goods, usually on very generous credit terms. This often allowed local merchants to supply rural customers with the latest products available in more urban locations.

Private Brands: By the 1870s, wholesale territories increasingly overlapped, intensifying the competition. Hardware distributors began putting their own brand names on merchandise they sold, especially cutlery, a very profitable, high-value line. This helped to develop brand loyalty with both consumers and retailers.

By World War I, there were dozens of private hardware, house-cutlery brands across the United States and Canada. Most were local or regional, but some were better known nationally than most manufacturers' brands, and these are highly collectable today. Some collectors specialize in obscure brands, or those from their own city or region. Private-brand pocket cutlery for hardware houses was usually made by contract manufacturers in the United States and Germany, since the United States Tariff Act of 1891 barred Sheffield cutlery firms from producing for the American market. This was one of the reasons that thousands of Sheffield and Solingen cutlers emigrated from England to

Below Belknap Hardware "John Primble" — Brand muskrat.

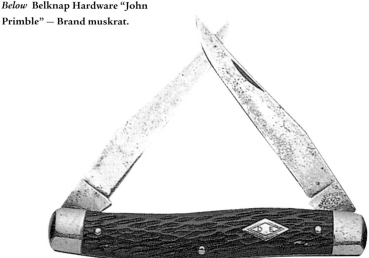

CUTLERY WHOLESALERS

Specialized wholesale cutlery firms played almost as large a role in American cutlery distribution as the wholesale hardware companies did. Prior to the Civil War, there were dozens of firms, selling English, German, and American cutlery to retailers and wholesalers across the United States. Since World War II, specialized cutlery wholesaling has continued to prosper. Some wholesale firms promote their own private brands, but most distribute a variety of widely advertised manufacturers' brands. The most important cutlery wholesaler firms include the following:

Boker: The oldest American wholesale cutlery firm still in business today is Heinrich Boker & Co., established in 1837 by German immigrants in New York. It has branches in Canada, Germany, and Mexico, and has its own factories in Solingen and New Jersey.

Kastor: The largest American wholesaler was Adolph Kastor &

Bros., founded in 1876. Its Germania Cutlery Works in Solingen operated as a factor commissioning American-style cutlery, to be made by Solingen craftsmen and factories. In 1902, Kastor bought and expanded the Camillus Cutlery Co. as a source of tariff-free, American-made knives; in addition to the many brands produced under Camillus' name, Kastor trademarks included Clover, Imperial Razor Co., Cutwell, Germania, A. W. Wadsworth, Ebro, Pathfinder, and Big Chief. Most of these brands were last used in 1947.

Wiebusch & Hilger: In 1864, William Hilger and Frederick Wiebusch bought factories in Sheffield, Germany, and Nixdorf, Bohemia, later building the Challenge Cutlery Co. in Bridgeport, Connecticut. Their brands included Atlantic, Western, Monumental, Walter Bros., Princeton, Owl, and Challenge. Charles Wiesbusch's extensive and unmatched knife collection is now in the Smithsonian Institution.

the United States. Since 1922, the dominant American pocketknife contractor has been Camillus, followed by Utica, Queen, and Alcas (makers of Cutco household knives).

Remington and the Demise of the United States Wholesale Hardware Business: When Remington Arms entered the pocketknife business it did not do any private-brand work, but pioneered global marketing of their own Remington UMC brand. As a result, hardware houses in every state and nation abandoned their house brands in favor of the pre-sold Remington line.

The Depression weeded out the weaker, less flexible hardware houses, the ones that were undercapitalized or that failed to adapt to changing times. It also bankrupted Remington, which had extended credit to all of the houses, but the company was saved when it was taken over by DuPont in 1933. What really killed the wholesale hardware business was World War II, which amounted to four long years of virtually zero business. Moreover, Remington, which had, until then, been a mainstay, abruptly dropped out of the cutlery business in 1940, leaving a vacuum that no other knife firm was able to fill. Even the strong hardware firms that did manage to survive the war, found the whole world, and its markets, changed after 1945 — diversity and high quality had nearly vanished from cutlery manufacture; markets were flooded with military-surplus knives; once-famous brand names had been forgotten by the fickle public; and the population, in general, was concentrating on the bigger cities and their suburbs.

Left Boker $2^3/_4$ in ($6^3/_4$ cm), all metal handles, etched Girl Scout, emblem on handle, one blade.

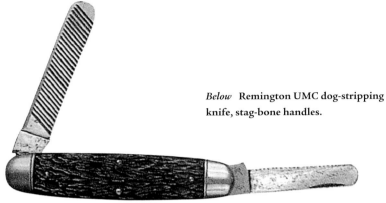

Below Remington UMC dog-stripping knife, stag-bone handles.

English Brands

Although the pocket-cutlery industry developed in England long before the American Revolution, from that time until 1891, its fortunes were inextricably intertwined with that of the United States. Despite the Revolution, Sheffield remained the American source for most of its high-quality cutlery, blade, spring, and tool steel, steel-making technology and capital, and thousands of skilled workmen. In return, America was Sheffield's largest export market.

The steep tariffs introduced by the United States in 1891 put an end to this mutually beneficial trading relationship, as many of Sheffield's premier pocket-cutlery firms were hurt by this additional burden. Nevertheless, the American pocket cutlery trade was indelibly affected by its links with Sheffield, which has helped to increase the city's fame in the posterity of pocketknife production.

George Wostenholm & Son – I*XL:
George Wostenholme originally founded this cutlery company near Sheffield, in 1745. His business was passed on to his grandson, George, who shortened the family name to Wostenholm, and continued producing cutlery in the Rockingham Works workshop in Sheffield. It was George's son (who was also called George) who registered the famous I *XL (I excel) trademark in 1826, and in 1830, sent a consignment of his cutlery with a leading factor and exporter, Naylor & Sanderson, to investigate the growing American markets. This venture proved so successful that the Wostenholms decided to concentrate all their efforts on creating cutlery for the United States, and subsequently moved the firm into a very large and modern factory called the Washington Works. They also made frequent visits to the United States to

promote their wares, as well as retaining an office in New York. The strategy paid off, for in a few years, Wostenholm's I*XL became the best-selling brand in the United States.

Joseph Rodgers & Sons — Star-Cross: In the nineteenth century, the best-known brand of cutlery in the world was Joseph Rodgers & Sons of Sheffield. Their famous Star-Cross trademark (a six-pointed star trademark, along with the Maltese cross, were granted to a family member in 1882, hence the name Star-Cross) may have been the first brand to achieve global recognition, and the company's name was, for a time, synonymous with the very best. In 1820, John Rodgers won a royal warrant, which allowed the firm to add the royal cipher to its mark, which further aided its reputation as the best-known pocket cutlery brand throughout the British Empire.

Rodgers-Wostenholm/Richards-Schrade: In 1971, two long-term Sheffield rivals Wostenholm and Rodgers merged to form one company. This company was later absorbed by Richards Bros., and finally purchased by Imperial-Schrade in 1977. The company was then moved into the largest, most modern plant in Sheffield, where the SCHRADE-I*XL

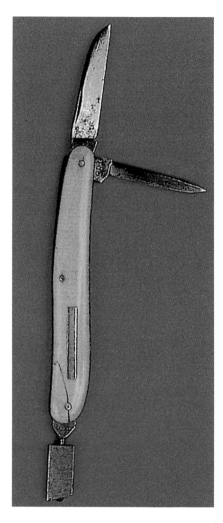

Above **Ivory-handled shadow-wharncliffe knife by John Nowill & Sons of Sheffield, incorporating a folding diamond-glass cutter by Sharrat & Newth.**

pocketknives were produced and subsequently marketed to American collectors. When the company went into receivership, all the Rodgers and Wolstenholm trademarks were sold to the Eggington Group, a small manufacturing firm based in Sheffield that produces pocketknives and cutlery for the United Kingdom.

While Rodgers and Wostenholm were the English cutlery firms best known outside the United Kingdom, many other cutlery firms based in Sheffield were equally well known within the British Isles.

Thomas Turner & Company: This company was founded in 1802, and moved to Norfolk Street in the 1820s. In 1834, the firm opened its Suffolk Works to make cutlery, tools, and crucible steel. By 1905, Turner was employing roughly 1,000 men, but the firm went out of business in 1932.

Mappin Brothers: This company began as the engraving firm of Joseph Mappin in 1810, and started to make cutlery in about 1820. In 1851, the firm moved to the Queen's Cutlery

Below I*XL, George Wostenholm, Sheffield, four-blade shadow senator genuine stag handles.

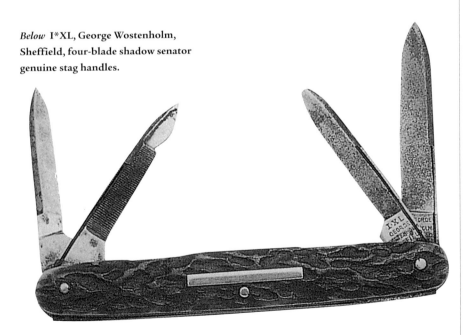

Works, where its multiblade sportsman's knives were a specialty, along with several thousand pocketknife patterns. In 1902, an allied firm called Mappin & Webb, absorbed the company. Thereafter, the alliance increasingly specialized in producing plated wares and jewelry.

Unwin & Rodgers (c1828–1867):
This company was best known for the knife that has become commonly known as the "patented pistol-knife."

Jonathan Crookes & Son — Heart-and-Pistol brand):
This firm was founded in 1780, and enjoyed a high reputation on both sides of the Atlantic.

Brookes & Crookes — Atlantic Works:
This company was founded in 1858 by Thomas Crookes and John Brookes. It specialized in manufacturing elaborate sportsman's knives as well as knives known as "ladies' knives".

Below G. Smith & Sons, Sheffield, horseman's knife with ivory handles, the integral bolster-liners and narrow square kicks indicate a knife made in Sheffield prior to c1860.

Harrison Brothers & Howson: This
company enjoyed royal patronage,
almost from its very foundation
in 1796. In 1847, some 50 years
after it was founded, the firm was
acquired by James W. Harrison,
William Howson, and Henry
Harrison, who opened American
agencies in New York as well as San
Francisco. Its Alpha Works remained
open until 1963.

George Ibberson & Co.: The company's
Violin pocketknives, registered in
1880, earned them high esteem. The
Ibberson family had been prominent
in Sheffield cutlery making since
1666; in 1914, Joseph Ibberson was
selected to harden and grind the first
stainless-steel knife blades. The firm
closed in 1988.

George Butler &Co.: This company's
Trinity Works was founded in 1768,
and enjoyed royal patronage. The
company is notorious for having
made, among other things, a 600-
piece, ivory-handled cutlery set for
the Prince of Wales in 1883. Though
still in business, Butler's last
pocketknives were made in 1972.
Butler trademarks included
Cavendish (named after a noble
patron). The knives are sold
principally in Britain, Australia,
India, and other former colonies.

Above **H. Kaufmann & Sons, Solingen,
spirit-level knife.**

German Brands

Since the late Middle Ages, the city
of Solingen in Germany has been
a center of steel and blade
manufacture, although it was
dependent on the older and larger
Cologne for much of its trade.
However, a rigid guild structure
limited the production of Solingen
cutlery for the European and world
markets. This system was halted when
cutlery merchant Peter Daniel Peres
was granted a charter by Duke
Maximilian of Bavaria, to erect the
city's first water-powered pocketknife
factory in 1805. Maximilian traded
with Napoleon, who abolished all
monopolies and privileges of the
Solingen guilds, thus clearing the way
for the rapid development of the
city's sword-and-cutlery industry.

Solingen's cutlery merchants sought to export internationally, and their goods were so competitively priced that even tariffs could not keep them out of the United States. By 1900, Solingen's cutlery exports exceeded those of the United States, England, and France combined.

Unfortunately, World War I closed world markets to German cutlery from 1915 to the 1920s, by which time American firms were already dominating the cutlery industry. World War II also destroyed much of the Solingen cutlery industry, and although it is still healthy today, it is only a shadow of its former self.

Above **W R. Case & Sons plier knife with bone handles; contract made by Boker Valley Forge.**

Heinrich Bolker & Co, — Tree Brand: In 1837, brothers Hermann and Robert Boker, partners in the sword-making business in Solingen, immigrated to North America. Hermann started H. Boker & Co. in New York City, importing cutlery, tools, and steel from Germany and England. Robert went to Mexico City, and founded Casa Roberto Boker. Their cousin, Heinrich Boker, opened a factory in 1869 in Solingen to manufacture Tree Brand pocketknives and cutlery for the brothers to sell. Heinrich also set up his own company in Solingen, and today Heinrich Boker & Co. is a leading private-brand contractor.

Above **Boker Tree Brand muskrat.**

H. Boker & Sons/Valley Forge Cutlery Co.: H. Boker & Sons, like other importers confronted with the United States Tariff Act of 1891, sought domestic sources of high-quality pocket cutlery, and in 1899, bought the Valley Forge Cutlery Co. in Newark, New Jersey. Both Boker and Valley Forge brand knives were made there, as well as private brands for other distributors. H. Boker & Sons was sold and acquired by various companies until all United States rights to Boker trademarks were resold to Heinrich Boker in Solingen. Boker's American sales office in Golden, Colorado now sells an up-to-date range of German pocket cutlery.

Swiss Cutlery

Victorinox/Wenger: Victorinox and Wenger are rival firms in Switzerland that both make red-handled, multiblade pocketknives for the Swiss army. Victorinox was created in 1884 by Karl Elsener, who joined his mother's name, Victoria, with inoxydable, which is French for "stainless" to form the company's name. The original Swiss Army Knife officer's model of 1897 was the prototype of all commercial versions, a six-blade utility knife with red, manmade handles.

Below **Victorinox Super Timer, Classic, and tie pin models.**

Edged Weapons from the East

China
India
Indonesia
Japan
Nepal

China

One of the great Chinese military philosophers of all time, Sun Tzu, advanced the art of warfare in China well before the sixth century BCE. However, weaponry seems to have been of only moderate quality, and military strength depended more on the number of chariots available than the actual art of warfare. Moreover, Chinese soldiers appear to have been valued more for their numbers than for their individual skills, an approach that produced few edged weapons of interest.

In recent times, among the weapons that fascinate are the Chinese execution swords, especially those used by the Manchu dynasty (1644–1912). Also of interest are the smaller blades, used by Chinese soldiers from the mainland and Taiwan.

The Mongol tribe of east-central Asia has become synonymous with military might. The name first appeared in Chinese records of the sixth century, but the power of the tribe reached its zenith under Genghis Khan, who became emperor in 1206, and his grandson, Kublai Khan (1216–94), the first Mongol emperor of China. The basic fighting unit of the Mongols was the touman, a 10,000-strong group. Their success was due to the use of signal flags, careful strategy, fanatical courage, and the fact that the Mongols were accustomed to hardship.

Although the Mongols were horsemen, their preferred arms were the bow, javelin, and lasso. It seems that, though it was poorly depicted in ancient illustrations, the Mongols did also carry a weapon that resembled a small scimitar or large saber. This weapon may, in fact, be the forerunner of the Indian talwar, but few edged weapons have ever been attributed to the Mongols.

Right **Early nineteenth century Chinese sword with a carved jade hilt and scabbard of *cloisonné* enamel.**

Far Right **Late eighteenth century (Ch'ing dynasty) Chinese sword. The mounts are of gilt copper and the scabbard is covered with green ray skin.**

India

The military heritage of the Indian subcontinent can be traced back to the original Aryan invasions, which occurred sometime between 2000 and 1000 BCE. These settlers from central Asia moved into the Punjab and the upper valley of the Ganges, bringing with them the rudiments of Hinduism.

The subcontinent, apart from the far south, was united under the Mauryan emperors who reigned from (321–184 BCE). The area was not unified again until the era of the Gupta dynasty (6000–500), whose rule was ended by the raids of the White Huns, which plunged India into anarchy.

During the eleventh and twelfth centuries, India suffered invasions from Muslims, Turks, Arabs, and Afghans. In 1206, the first Muslim dynasty was established, which was followed by three centuries of Muslim rule throughout the north and the Deccan. In the fourteenth to sixteenth

Left Gold-encrusted northern Indian sword (khanda), fitted with an early seventeenth century, European broadsword blade. The hilt and mounts may date from the seventeenth century, but were probably redecorated around 1800.

Left Jade-hilted Indian sword
(talwar), richly set with gold,
rubies, emeralds, and diamonds;
damascened in gold on the blade,
with the name and badge
(a tiger) of Tipu Sultan, "Tiger of
Mysore," who was killed in 1799
by British troops.

centuries, the south remained independent under the Hindu Vijayanagar dynasty. The greatest period of Muslim India began in 1527, with the founding of the Mogul empire by Babur. Although officially lasting until 1858, this empire fell into decline after 1707 when traders from Portugal, Holland, France, and Britain began to establish outposts in India. Within a century, British rule was established throughout the subcontinent.

India has, therefore, seen much warfare, but technologically, appears to have lagged behind other areas. Iron weapons did not appear until

Right An illuminated manuscript from the mid-seventeenth century that depicts a battle between Persian and Indian forces, probably somewhere in the northern part of the subcontinent. Most of the weapons then popular with both nationalities are on display.

Below This piece of art was done by an anonymous Indian artist and shows a scene from the horrible Sepoy Mutiny of 1857–58.

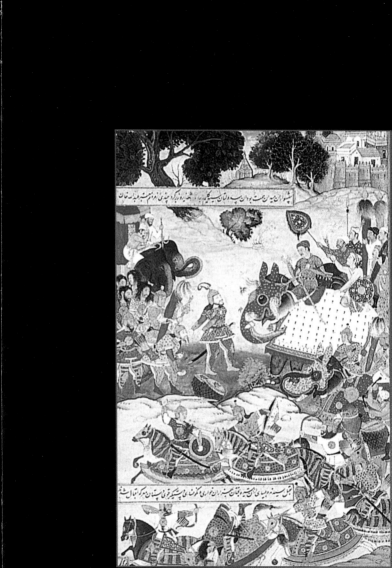

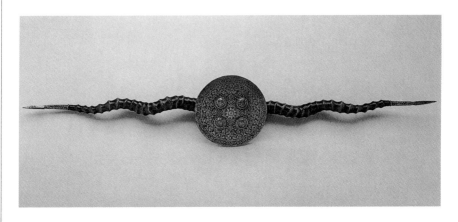

around 500 BCE, when chariots were the basis of military strength. The infantry was largely composed of bowmen, and India's greatest military treatise, the *Siva-Dhanur-Veda*, which appeared around 500 CE, concentrated on archers. Hand-to-hand conflict was on the whole avoided, and by 200 CE Hindu conflict was conducted along essentially ritual lines, with limited objectives sought and mass-slaughter avoided. Nevertheless, an astonishing variety of interesting edged weapons was produced in the subcontinent. One of the most curious was the *bagh nakh* ("tiger's claw"), a five-pronged weapon that slipped over the hand like brass knuckles.

Collecting weapons from the Indian subcontinent was not difficult. This is mostly due to the fact that most of the maharajahs

Above A set of fakir's horns, clearly showing the metal tips projecting from the horns of bone.

Right An Indian nobleman leading troops into battle in central India, c1700. His pata is quite distinct. Other weaponry indicates that the scene dates from the Mogul period, when swords essentially replaced archery. However, the two men (left rear) each appear to be carrying a koras, the national sword of Nepal. It can therefore only be assumed that the two men were mercenaries, or that the artist was exercising considerable license.

established extensive collections, and dealers and tourists could acquire examples easily. This is still possible, but prices have increased. The most desirable Indian weapons include the bichwa, khanjarli, and pata.

Bhuj

The characteristic Hindu dagger of northern India is known as the bhuj, or kutti. It is also sometimes called the elephant knife, as a motif of the animal often features as a decoration on the weapon. The single-edged blade was comparatively heavy, although only 7–10in (17–25cm) long. A decorative knob served as a pommel. The bhuj was unusual, as its long tang could be screwed into a hollow hilt, thereby transforming the blade into a sword.

Bichwa

The word *bichwa* means "sting of the scorpion." Having come into popular use in the seventeenth century, this dagger has since attracted a certain amount of legend, because it was the preferred weapon of assassins. The blade was formed in the precise configuration of a buffalo horn, and a steel hilt was usually looped around it to make a knuckleguard, and to afford greater strength and security. The blade length was 10in (25cm).

Jambiya

This single-edged knife is a very attractive weapon. The blade was often inlaid with gold, jade, or ivory, and the wooden sheaths, which tended to be much longer than the blades, were embossed

Left Indian bichwa dagger for the right hand. It is damascened with silver, and dates from the nineteenth century.

Right "Fakir's crutch" (*zafar takia*), concealing a 19in (47cm) blade. The handle is of agate, jade, and other semiprecious stones; Indian, nineteenth century.

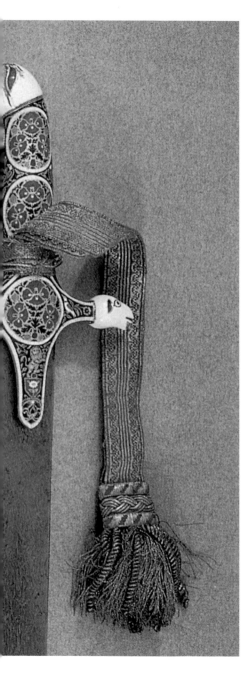

with leather or silk. The knife was the symbol of a free man, and to have it taken away meant irredeemable degradation. The jambiya blade could be from 5–10in (12–25cm) in length. Shorter models were preferred in India; the longest known ones were used by the Berbers in Morocco. These weapons are still manufactured, but only for ornamental purposes.

Kard

This single-edged, rather unpretentious weapon could be anything from 8–16in (20–40cm) long. The tip was thickened to increase the effectiveness of the blow. The grip was of bone or horn, and the straight hilt had no hand guard.

Khanda

If India can be said to have a national sword, it is the khanda. It has a long, straight blade with a blunt point. The blade was generally single-edged and wider at the tip. The padded grip inclined forward, and a curved spike formed a pommel, allowing the khanda to be used in much the same way as the European bastard sword.

Left **Gold and enamel mounted Indian swords, dating from the early nineteenth century. The guards bear the crest of the East India Company.**

Khanjar

The khanjar is, like the talwar, of
Muslim origin, and some variant of
the word means knife in several
languages. The khanjar blade was
9–12in (23–30cm) long, double-
edged, and slightly curved. Pistol-
shaped grips were usually made of
jade or ivory, and the swords were
very often inlaid with gold and
colored stones.

Khanjarli

The khanjarli blade is distinct
because of the particular curvature
of its blade. The 5–10in (13–25cm)
long blade first sweeps upward,
and then appears to straighten out.
The blade was accompanied with or
without knuckleguards.The hilts
were most often made of ivory, and
the pommel was fan-shaped.

Left Khanjar handle dating from c1800. This handle was carved from a solid piece of rock crystal.

Right Early nineteenth century Indian Mogul dagger, the khanjar, carved with jade hilt and carefully enameled to resemble precious stones.

Pata

Exclusively a Hindu weapon, the pata had a long, straight, usually double-edged blade. Because it became popular at the time when European traders were establishing themselves in India, the blades were usually made in Italy or Spain. The pata was accompanied by a metal attachment that protected the arm holding the weapon, thus making it into a gauntlet sword. Although using patas was a difficult technique to master, skilled pata swordsmen were among the best swordsmen the subcontinent ever produced.

Talwar

Perhaps the most respected of Indian edged weapons was the talwar, which is believed to have originated with the Mongols, who brought it to India during the sixteenth century. The blade was deeply curved and tapered continuously to the tip, and was decorated with floral designs and personal inscriptions. The scabbard, which was usually of wood, was suspended from the belt by rings.

Right Nineteenth century talwar with hilt damascened with gold.

Far Right Mahratta (Southern Indian) gauntlet sword, or pata, from the seventeenth century; the blade is earlier (sixteenth century), and imported from Europe.

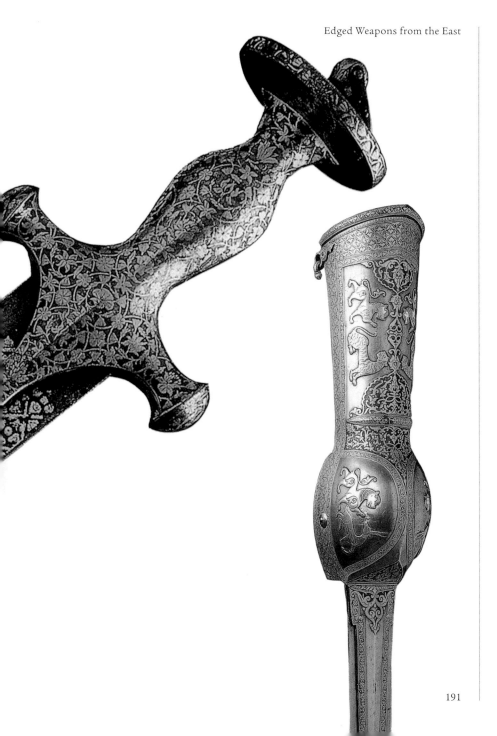

Indonesia

The area we now know as Indonesia saw considerable military activity. The first great military power was the kingdom of Srividjaya in southern Sumatra, which existed in the fifth century. Thereafter, various powers came and went. Despite its fragmented history, however, the area has produced some notable edged weapons.

Kris

The kris, or malay dagger, is undoubtedly one of the best known and most effective weapons. The kris, associated with the King of Janggolo (a Muslim sultanate in central Java), is believed to have originated in the fourteenth century, but its history is shrouded in myth — indeed, local tradition avers that a good kris has a soul of its own.

The shape of the blade varied widely. However, despite the shape, it was always formed from three layers of soft

steel or iron, with thinner layers in between. It was then beaten or twisted into shape. The blades were usually double-edged and 12–16in (30–41cm) long, although executioners' kris daggers from Java were 24in (60cm) long. The kris was almost invariably decorated with engravings depicting dragons and demons. A ring called uwar, fitted between the blade and the hilt, formed a primitive handguard. This provided additional decoration and a means of suspending the weapon from a belt. Kris daggers were usually kept in elaborately decorated scabbards embossed with brass, tortoise-shell motifs, or painted figures.

Today, collectors should find few problems collecting kris daggers, as they are still made in Southeast Asia, and are reasonably priced.

Below **Magnificent late seventeenth century Malayan kris, the hilt of carved ivory depicting the Hindu god Vishnu; the scabbard is overlaid with intricately worked gold, the gold chape and hilt socket further enriched with cabochon rubies.**

Wedong

One of the most fascinating weapons that originated from Indonesia was the wedong. Resembling an elongated butcher's cleaver because of the sweeping lines that occur along the cutting edge, the wedong was primarily used as a chopping weapon. It is not impossible to acquire examples of this weapon today, although antique varieties of the wedong are considered very difficult to find.

Mandau

The mandau is an all-purpose blade used by several tribal groups in Indonesia. The word means "head hunter," as it was used for that very purpose for centuries. The blade is usually single-edged, up to 20in (50cm) long, and slightly curved. Hand guards are rare, but the pommels are carved to represent ornate masks or figures.

Above nineteenth-century Java kris, entirely overlaid with embossed and chased sheet silver.

Right Silver mounted knife from the Malay Peninsula, probably Javanese; mid-nineteenth century.

Japan

Until about the fifthth century CE, Japanese history remained shrouded in mystery. In recent times, Jimmu Tenno, the leader of the Asiatic invaders and long-regarded folk hero, was accorded official status as Japan's first ruler. In the fifth century, the art of writing was introduced from Korea, and in the sixth century, Chinese culture became generally accepted, although attempts in the seventh century to establish a strong, centralized, Chinese-style monarchy to limit the power of the nobles failed, and real power was retained in the hands of the great feudal families, the daimyos (or daimios).

In the twelfth century, a feudal military caste known as the samurai assumed power. The word, which means "guard," originally applied to those who bore arms, but was eventually restricted to the warrior knights and administrators who became retainers of the daimyos. The samurai remained in power until the fall of Tokugawa shogunate in 1867. They obeyed the bushido code (the way of the warrior), which was derived from a mixture of religious beliefs, social obligations, and civic consciousness. Its basic tenets of bravery, honor, and service dictated that a worthy warrior would be ready to die without warning, with unsullied honor and memory.

In 1192 the ruling noble Yoritomo assumed the title shogun (commander in chief), a title that was borne until 1867 by the real ruler of Japan. During the fifteenth and sixteenth centuries, Japan sank into a state of feudal anarchy, from which it was rescued between 1570 and 1615 by three great shoguns — Nobunaga, Hideyoshi, and Ieyasu. It was the family of the last of these, the Tokugawa, which continued to wield power, until the emperor Meiji reasserted the power of the throne in 1867 and abolished the shogunate. During the next 30 years, the privileges of the nobility were abolished, a uniform code of law was introduced, and a constitution was established.

The cult of the samurai has continued to exert fascination, and by extention, so have the swords

Right **Fabled Shogun Ieyasu at Sekigahara (Barrier Field). Waged in 1600, this crucial battle foreshadowed the Edo period, which made Tokyo predominant in Imperial affairs.**

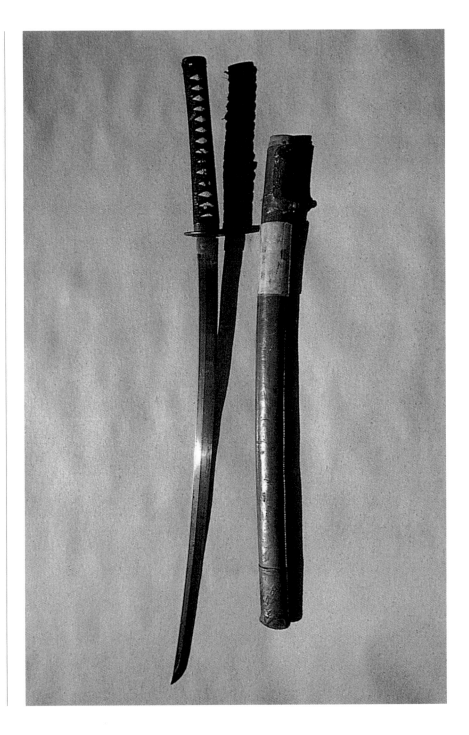

associated with this era. The samurai's code was based on the veneration of the sword. Weapons were called nippon-to (soul of the samurai), and sword makers were held in high esteem. Today, Japan has designated 77 individuals who excel in traditional crafts; several of which are weapon makers. Nippon-to are divided into four categories: the first, ka-to, includes antiques of great value; the second, shin-t, comprise weapons made between 1700 and 1877; the third group, shinshin-to, includes weapons made between 1877 and the beginning of World War II; and the fourth group, gun-to, includes mass-produced weapons issued to officers and non-commissioned personnel during World War II.

Amongst Japan's most prized edged weapons are the daisho, haikuchi, nagamaki, hamidashi, tachi, and no-dachi. Some smaller weapons appear at auction and through dealers, but collectors should be aware that chances of legally acquiring examples of swords, except gun-to, are remote.

Left **Historic samurai swords outside Japan are quite rare. This version of the katana, from a private American collection, dates from c1700, and is apparently a shin-to weapon.**

Daisho

The daisho were principal arms of the samurai. The daisho actually comprises two weapons, the main weapon was the long sword, the katana, while the second, originally called the tanto, was the wakizashi. The blade of a katana was 25–32in (63–82cm) long, although some of those made before 1700 were shorter. The wakizashi was smaller, but not by a great deal: its average length was 15–18in (38–45cm).

Daisho were formed of a soft iron, alloyed with several prescribed grades of steel. During manufacture, most of the blade was covered in a special paste of clay, sand, and charcoal, leaving exposed the cutting edge, the yakiba. Many sets of daisho, especially examples of the katana, are still found outside Japan, but with great difficulty and at a high cost.

Haikuchi

Sometimes also known as *aikuchi*, the haikuchi is amongst the best known of the plethora of shorter blades used in Japan. The name can be translated as "pleasant companion," but the actual weapon was deadly. The hilt was usually wood with horn fittings, while the blades were 8–10in (20–25cm) long. These weapons became popular in the nineteenth century.

Hamidashi

The Japanese equivalent of the
dirk, the hamidashi was an
impressive weapon. It had a single-
edged, slightly curved blade, about
8–12in (20–30cm) long. The hilt
was usually bound with plaited
cords over a covering of fish skin.
For centuries, the hamidashi
enjoyed a reputation as the
assassin's favored weapon.

Kwaiken

This interesting blade was an old-
fashioned dagger designed for
women. With a double-edged blade
about 8–12in (20–30cm) in length, it
could be used defensively. The
kwaiken was also apparently used for
seppuku, or ritual suicide by
hara-kiri, if a woman faced disgrace.

Nagamaki

A two-handed weapon somewhat akin
to a halberd, the nagamaki could be
attached to a shorter handle, and
used as a sword. It became popular in
about 1600, and continued to be
widely used even during the
restructuring of Japanese society,

**Right Japanese sword (katana) of the early
nineteenth century; the blade, however,
dates from the late fifteenth century, and
was made by the Mihara school of
swordsmiths, Bingo Province.**

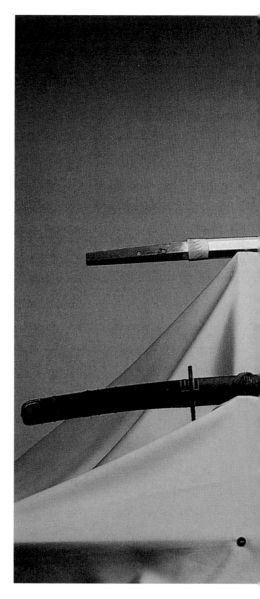

which began in 1867. Soldiers who wanted to use it had to be specially trained. Although a few nagamaki are thought to be in collections outside Japan, but they are unlikely to be available for sale.

No-dachi

Although it never achieved widespread acceptance among soldiers in Japan, one of the weapons that appears most in Japanese art is the no-dachi, or field sword. These enormous weapons, with blades often as long as 6ft (2m), were carried across the backs of soldiers. Special echelons of soldiers were trained specifically to use it, as it was instrumental in launching spearhead attacks, which were essential in order to break open enemy lines. The no-dachi was strictly a fighting weapon, and bears little decoration as a result, with scabbards made of plain wood. However, because few no-dachi were ever made, they are difficult to locate and collect.

Tachi

The tachi is, perhaps, the most historic of all Japanese edged weapons, as was the original sword of the samurai. The blades were usually 24–28in (60–70cm) long, although some later examples were 20–24in (50–60cm) long. The tachi was hung edge downward from the belt by two straps. The scabbard was made of wood overlaid with metal, and both the sword's hilt and scabbard were decorated with floral and mythical motifs. Although the daisho eventually replaced the tachi as the preferred weapon of the samurai, the tachi remained the weapon that was worn at court and on ceremonial occasions. Today, it is virtually impossible for a collector of oriental weaponry to legally acquire a tachi.

Right Japanese dirk
(wakizashi); of the late
eighteenth century.
Far Right Japanesse dirk of
the nineteenth century.

Left Late eighteenth
century tachi.

Nepal

Nepal has produced some of the greatest warriors of recent times. The country developed as a group of feudal kingdoms, though the Gurkhas established modern Nepal in 1769. In 1815, after prolonged battle, Nepal was subjugated by Britain, and the Gurkhas were recruited into the British Army, in which, until recently, as many as 80,000 fearless fighters continued to serve.

Khukri

The khukri, or kukri, is the knife carried by the Gurkhas. It has a forward-angled blade with a pistol-grip hilt. The blade is heavy, single-edged, and weighted towards the point, allowing a blow of maximum impact to be delivered with minimum effort. The straight hilt is usually made of wood or ivory, there is no hand guard, and the pommel is disk-shaped. Smaller blades are also sometimes carried in sheath, although the khukri itself was used for chopping almost anything from necks to firewood.

During World War II, a curious scene perplexed many Allied soldiers. A Gurkha would always let anyone look at the blade of his khukri, but before returning it to its sheath, he would always prick his finger with it. This was done because of a local tradition, which stated that a weapon could not return to its sheath by a living Gurkha, without tasting blood!

Kora

The national sword of Nepal is actually the kora, which dates from the nineth century. The distinctive blade, which is approximately 24in (60cm) long, curves inward and has concave incisions in the tip. The lower tip incision always depicts the Buddhist symbol of a lotus flower surrounded by a circle. Today, the hilt is usually made of steel, although it is possible to find older examples with brass hilts. The grip is tubular, and is held between two disk-shaped objects. Scabbards are fashioned in leather and decorated with embroidered velvet.

Right **Ghurka knife (khukri) mounted with silver, c1800, along with smaller blades, which would have been carried in the sheath. The particularly fine blade is of damascus watered steel.**

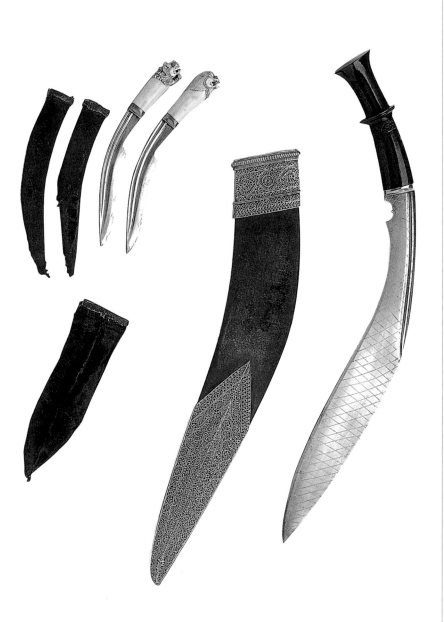

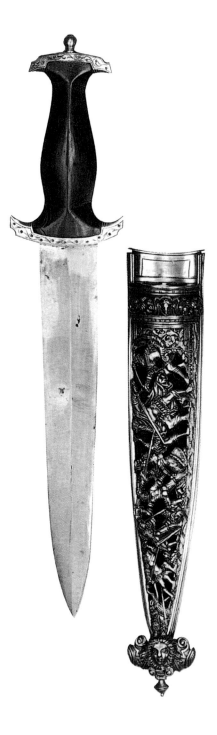

Collection
and Care

Collection and Care

It might be thought that only recent weapons can be collected in the traditional sense. It is, of course, true that the older the weapon, the more expensive and difficult it will be to acquire. Yet, it is possible to obtain such pieces. Private and aristocratic collections are dispersed from time to time, and interesting and unusual articles constantly appear on the market.

In 1990, an auction at Sotheby's in London included a display on the extremely rare Lloyd's Patriotic Fund presentation sword, an early fifteenth century Italian weapon, and a British cavalry saber, which may have been used at Waterloo. This display, at only one of the world's auction houses, is evidence to the fact that collector's swords, knives, and daggers — even those that are rare — are still available.

However, before spending any money at all, collectors should gather as much information as possible through museums, books, and auction house resources. Collectors can, for example, visit museums and exhibitions that showcase militaria and edged weapons. Reading up as much as possible on the subject also helps to establish a worthy collection. Books, journals, magazines, and historical manuscripts provide valuable research on edged weapons. The American publisher, House of Collectibles, in Orlando, Florida, produces a large number of books on all aspects of collecting, including knives and other edged weapons. It is also important to establish contact with dealers and auction houses, most of which are reputable; indeed, dishonest dealers quickly go out of business!

Money Matters

Collecting is a hobby that can be considerably expensive. Even the cheapest historic weapon is not something that one is likely to acquire on a credit card. It is, of course, an insoluble problem. Some feel cheated if they pay a certain amount for an object and find that, a year later, they could obtain it for less somewhere else. This dilemma is intrinsic to the nature of collecting. The prices of collectables are determined by the laws of supply and demand: what a particular weapon is worth depends on what the seller can get for it, and what the buyer will give at any particular time.

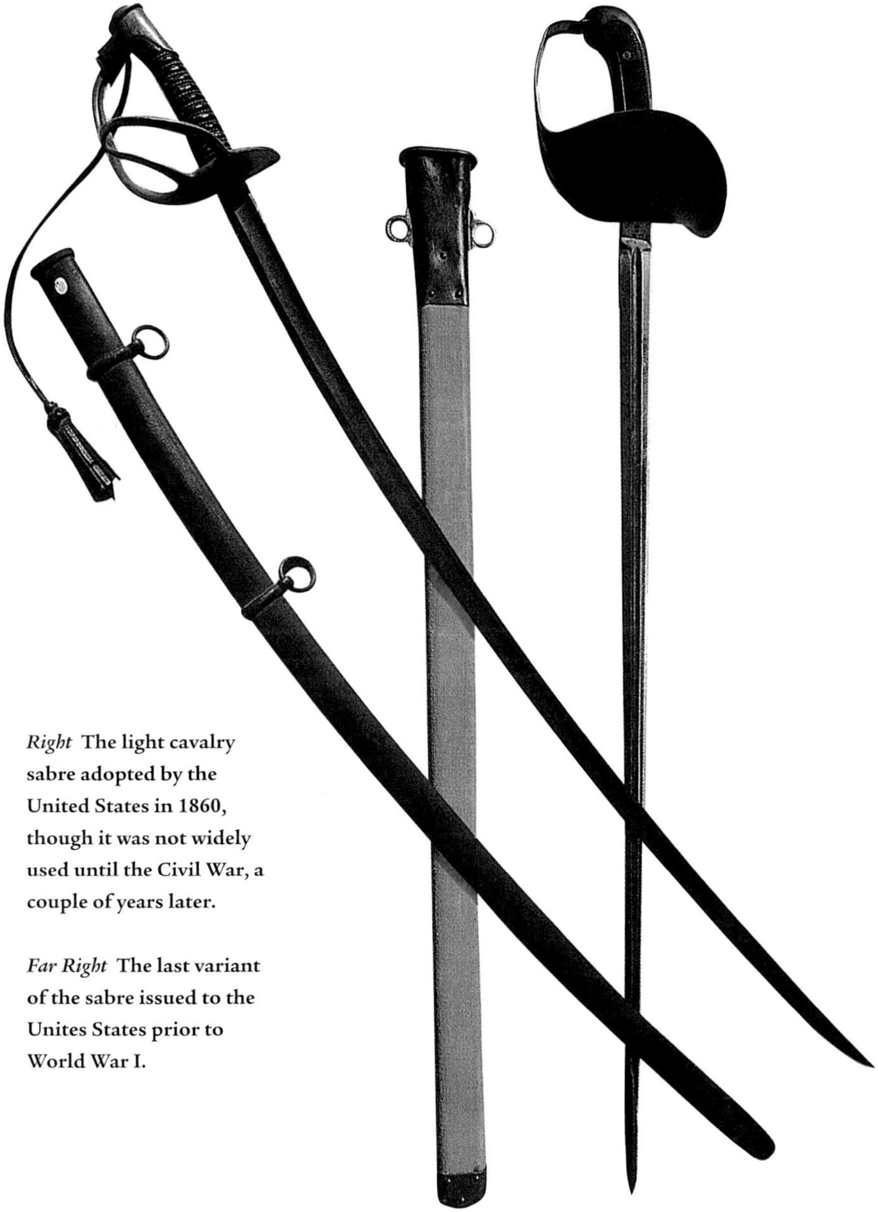

Right The light cavalry
sabre adopted by the
United States in 1860,
though it was not widely
used until the Civil War, a
couple of years later.

Far Right The last variant
of the sabre issued to the
Unites States prior to
World War I.

Far Right In the early nineteenth century, Lloyd's of London distributed presentation swords like this one to British military figures who performed exemplary service. The normal cost of such a weapon at the time was not less than 100 pounds sterling.

Below A French knight's sword belonging to the second half of the fourteenth century, the era of the 100 Years War. Its tapering double edge and relatively short length indicate that it was designed primarily for thrusting.

Taking Care

One of the first problems that collectors are faced with is security. It is wise never to make the contents of a collection known to anyone who is not completely trustworthy. Arranging the collection on a wall for people to see is not wise either. In fact, it is often worthwhile to install some type of home security system to help ensure the safety of a collection.

Insurance is something that all collectors should become familiar with. It is impossible to suggest what sort of premiums one may have to pay, although they are likely to be high. Nevertheless, insuring one's collection is vital. Additionally, all weapons should be photographed, in color if possible, and from several angles, and any distinguishing marks should be photographed and listed separately.

The very nature of weapons means that they are far more durable than glass or porcelain. However, the greatest enemy of all metal weapons is moisture, which causes rust. Edged weapons must therefore be protected by their sheaths at all times and, if possible, stored under glass. Rust often starts to attack metal in small scratches and nicks. Polishing the blade carefully with a fine abrasive, and then covering it with Vaseline or oil keeps the moisture out. Edged

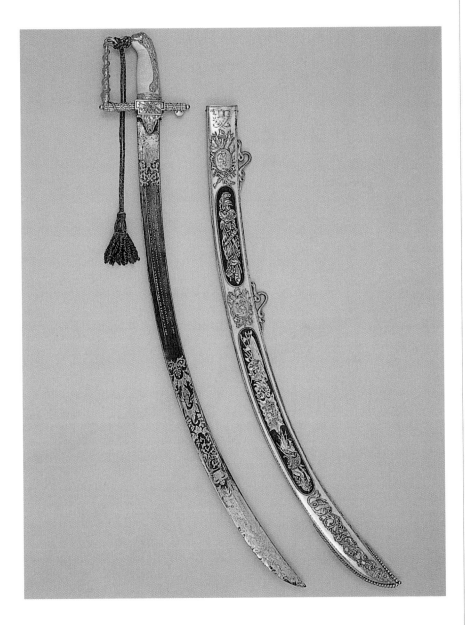

weapons should also be kept away from direct sunlight. Infrared rays can cause any non-metallic parts — wood, bone, or ivory handles, for instance — to fade, and this will detract from the weapon's appearance, and thus, its value.

Transporting a collection of edged weapons also requires special care. Collectors should avoid unwarranted attention or damage in transit. Some collectors advocate wrapping blades in oilcloth, however, specially treated leather cloth is available. Ordinary leather is not advisable, as it contains tanning acids that not only increase rusting, but also generate corrosion.

Above This weapon dates from c1750, before the American Revolution. It was probably once an infantry officer's sword. The weapon crossing over it is exactly a century younger. The inscribed "VR" (Victoria, Regina) indicates that it was from the nineteenth century.

Fakes and Forgeries

Fortunately, militaria haven't seemed to attract the fakers and forgers who have bedeviled other areas of collectables. Nevertheless, the best way to avoid making mistakes is to know as much as possible about the subject. A story that is often told to illustrate this point describes a wealthy Japanese investor who, upon visiting the United States, was propositioned by a local who wanted to sell a short sword to the visitor. The seller claimed he was destitute, and therefore willing to let the sword go for as little as 25,000USD, even though it was the very weapon with which the Japanese war leader and Prime Minister, Hideki Tojo, had committed hara-kiri at the end of World War II. The patriotic Japanese businessman quickly bought the sword as a matter of national pride. However, when he returned home, he learnt that Hideki Tojo had shot himself!

Before purchasing any weapon, it should be examined carefully. Do all the parts seem to belong together? Are the blade, hilt, and cross guard

Right **A nineteenth century copy of a Renaissance sword (perhaps based on the sword of Philip the Fair in Vienna); the blade, however, is an original Italian c1500.**

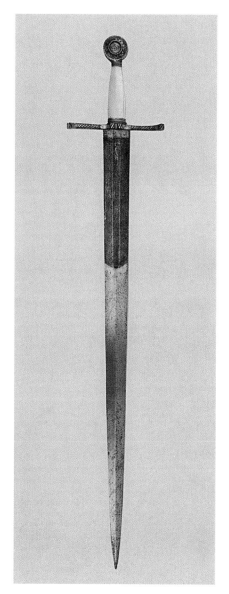

compatible and well placed? Does the handle look artificially aged, or falsly paired to an older blade? Are the conditions of the hilt and grip consistent?

Old engravings of the maker's mark or signature are also good indicators of a weapon's authenticity. Try to see if the marks have been properly put on. If they were lightly stamped or badly adhered, they can easily be excised with a sharp knife tip. Although nothing is invariable, as a general rule, identifying that marks and sword makers' signatures were put on the blade or tang before the weapon received its final heat treatment is important, because as such, they should not come off.

The blades of smaller weapons should be flexible. An old, brittle blade, attached to a weapon that is purportedly fairly new, may even splinter. In addition, the blade may not be properly seated within its new handle. The tang might not be properly formed to fit snugly inside — if it rattles, it is most probably fake. There is, however, no foolproof way of testing a blade on one's own — even experts sometimes fail on occasion.

Collectors should never risk paying for something they are unsure about. Although mistakes are inevitable, one must protect oneself from some basic errors. The scimitar, for example, was originally considered to be solely a combat weapon. There should normally be nothing but the name of the maker or owner, or a brief religious text engraved on it. If someone tries to sell a lavishly ornamented scimitar, for instance, a collector should be suspicious. One of the best ways to avoid problems of this kind is to buy through dealers, brokers, and auction houses, who employ experts to guide collectors to the right purchase. Such professionals depend on their carefully guarded reputation, and it is therefore never in their interest for a client to think he has been duped. At the same time, collectors should always beware of bargains. For example, anyone who is willling to sell a nineteenth century Bowie knife cheaply, is probably selling a fake knife.

A word about restoration: some people believe that if a weapon is not precisely the way it was made, it is not authentic. However, weapons can be repaired as long as authentic parts are used. Repair and restoration should always be left to experts and one should never try to straighten weakened metal, or glue pieces of an edged weapon together, as a badly repaired or restored item may be worth less than the damaged article.

Left A fake nineteenth century cinquedea dagger, the only original element of which is the pommel, which was once probably once two French sixteenth century knife handles.

Pocketknife Collecting

Considering the different types and brands of pocketknives available, it is important to pay attention to what other collectors may want and expect in order to have a commercially successful pocketknife collection.

Fashion

As a general comparison, pocketknife trends change more often in modern, handmade knives, and less in antique and classic knives.

This is because all that is required to start a fashion is for two free-spending collectors to compete for the same knives; if their rivalry persists for any length of time, other people will join, and prices will soon soar in that particular market niche.

Condition

Second in importance for collectors is the condition of the knife. A knife in excellent, unsharpened condition is worth much more than one in lesser condition, which knowledgeable collectors will not buy at any price. Moreover, if you clean or sharpen a knife to improve its appearance, you actually risk destroying much of its resale value.

Many collectors will only consider buying knives in perfect condition, which means knives that have never been used, carried, cleaned, or sharpened. While this holds especially true for modern knives, mint condition, antique pocketknives are a delicate subject because their materials are difficult to maintain — their blades and springs can rust, their fittings become discolored, or their handle materials shrink or crack. Despite these risks, there remains a strong market for antique knives in true mint condition.

Left NKCA (National Knife Collectors Association) 1992 Club Knife, trapper pattern made by Queen Cutlery Co.

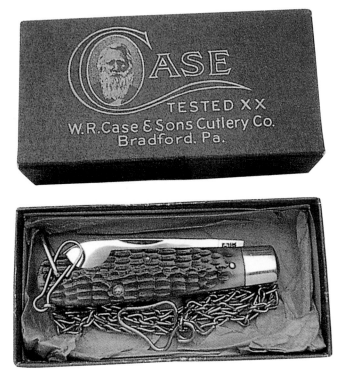

Above Case "Tested XX" easy-open, barehead, standard jack with shackle and chain, jigged-bone handles, and original box.

Below Reading is a good
way to further your
knowledge of pocketknives.
Among those pictured
here are *Levine's Guide*,
1985 edition (the 3rd
edition was published in
1993), and J. Bruce Voyle's
Antique Knives. Also
featured are popular knife
magazines—*Edges, Knife
Magazine,* and *Knife World.*

Cleaning

The rules of cleaning are simple: when in doubt, don't clean. Over enthusiastic cleaning will destroy whatever remains of a knife's original finish, which will substantially reduce its value. Also, a cautious buyer will assume that a heavily cleaned knife has been reworked, even if this is not the case. There are a few exceptions — fingerprints should be wiped off with a soft, clean cloth. A drop of light machine oil can be applied to the joint of each blade, but never lubricants containing solvents or dryers. Clean lint and grease using a wooden toothpick.

Top Row, left to right **Recent Schrade Barlow knife, smooth-bone handles; Parker Cutlery Co's miniature jackknife, abaloneshell handles; 1980s Case light trapper, red jigged-bone handles.**

Middle **Late nineteenth century, large Sheffield horseman's multiblade with stag handles, made for A. G. Alford Sporting Goods Co., Baltimore, MD.**

Bottom Row, left to right **Ka-Bar jackknife with razor and spey blades, wood handles; Case serpentine jack, genuine stag handles; Parker Cutlery Co. small lockback with pearl handles.**

Museums to Visit

Almost every country has at least one museum or institution where a major collection of edged weapons may be seen. The ones listed below are those whose collections are generally regarded as wide-ranging and historically complete.

Austria

Historisches Museum der Stadt Wien, Vienna

Landeszenghaus, Graz
Waffensammlung, Vienna

Belgium

Porte de Hal, Brussels

Czech Republic

Castle Collaredo-Mansfield, Opocno

Denmark

Tojhusmet, Copenhagen

France

Musée de l'Armée, Paris

Musée du Louvre, Paris

Musée Massena Joubert Collection, Nice

Germany

Historisches Museum, Dresden

Museum für Deutsche Geschichte, Berlin

Italy

Museo Nazionale, Florence

Museum Stibbert Collection, Florence

Netherlands

Rijksmuseum voor Volkenkunde, Leiden

Poland

Wawel Armoury, Cracow

Russia

State Hermitage Museum, St Petersburg

Spain

Armoury, Palacio Réal de Madrid, Madrid

Sweden

Kungl Livrustkammaren, Stockholm

Switzerland

Landesmuseum, Zurich

Historischemuseum, Basle

U.K.

The Armouries, Tower of London, London

Castle Museum, York

Fitzwilliam Museum, Cambridge

Imperial War Museum, London

Museum of London,
Barbican Centre,
London

Royal Scottish Museum,
Edinburgh

Wallace Collection,
Manchester Square,
London

Windsor Castle Museum,
Windsor

Victoria & Albert Museum,
London

USA
Allentown Art Museum,
Pennsylvania

Brooklyn Museum,
New York

*Chicago Museum of
History,* Illinois

City Art Museum,
St Louis, Missouri

Cleveland Museum of Art,
Ohio

*Metropolitan Museum of
Art,* New York

National Knife Museum,
Chattanooga,
Tennessee

Smithsonian Institution,
Washington DC

West Point Museum, West
Point,
New York

Left A Gentleman's Rapier (c1640–50), probably German. The blade is a German imitation of a Spanish style, and measures 39.5in (100cm).

Index

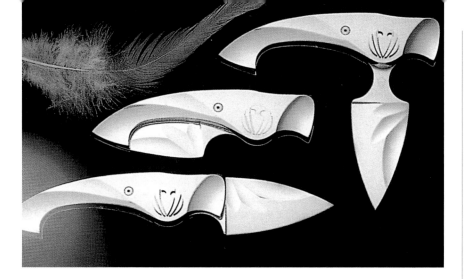